D0723584

3.50

# Celebrating the Word

# Celebrating the Word

*Ecumenical Insights by*
  *Godfrey Diekmann*
  *David Hay*
  *Eugene Fairweather*
  *Howard Hagemen*
  *Joseph Cunningham*

*Edited with an*
*Introduction by*
  *James Schmeiser*

**The third symposium of the
Canadian Liturgical Society,
"Worship '75"**

The Anglican Book Centre
Toronto, Canada

Copyright © 1977

The Anglican Book Centre
600 Jarvis Street
Toronto, Ontario
Canada M4Y 2J6

ISBN 0-919030-19-X

Printed and Bound by
**The Alger Press**
**Oshawa, Canada**

# Contents

# Contributors

Prof. James Schmeiser, King's College, London, Ontario; member of the board of directors, Canadian Liturgical Society.

The Rev. Godfrey Diekmann, O.S.B.; editor-in-chief of *Worship*; member of the board of directors, National Liturgical Conference of the Roman Catholic Church, U.S.A.

The Rev. Prof. David Hay, Knox College, Toronto; past chairman, Committee on Church Worship, Presbyterian Church of Canada.

The Rev. Prof. Eugene Fairweather, Keble professor of divinity, Trinity College, Toronto; world-renowned Anglican Scholar.

The Rev. President Howard Hageman, New Brunswick Theological Seminary, New Jersey; chairman, Worship Committee, Reformed Church of America.

The Rev. Joseph Cunningham, chairman, National Federation of the Diocesan Liturgical Commissions, Roman Catholic Church, U.S.A.

# Introduction

*James Schmeiser*

In 1969 a conference on worship was held at the University of Ottawa under the leadership of Professor Ernest Skublics. At the close of this conference a group of Canadians from all denominations met to consider how the interest in worship aroused by the conference could be maintained in Canada.

This led to the founding on 24 November 1969 of the Canadian Liturgical Society. It is a society which has no official authorization from the various denominations but has representatives on its board of directors from such major denominations as the Anglican Church of Canada, the Presbyterian Church in Canada, the Roman Catholic Church, the United Church of Canada, and the Baptist Church. It is a voluntary society of academically, professionally, pastorally, or otherwise interested individuals, for the promotion of study, information, development, and co-operation between the various Christian denominations in Canada, in the area of Christian worship. Membership in the society, however, has not been limited to those resident in Canada but includes others, mainly from the United States.

The aims and objectives of the society are as follows:

1. To serve as an organ of information on literature, periodicals, resource persons, organizations, conventions, study programmes, etc.

2. To spur interdisciplinary research, study, and publications in areas relevant to worship, such as language, culture, communications, media, art, architecture, music, the performing arts, and behavioural and social sciences, anthropology, history, theology, etc.

3. To serve the churches, other organs, scholars, and ministers as a consultative organ, studying, comparing, and commenting on new rites, pastoral developments and problems, etc.

4. To act if needed as a liaison between churches and other organs, such as councils, institutes, and societies in Canada and abroad.

5. To promote conventions, conferences, and seminars both on a regional and a national basis.

The main contribution of the society up to the present time has been in organizing seminars and conferences. In June 1972 a most successful conference on the theme of prayer was held at Saint Augustine's Seminary in Toronto.

In 1973 two seminars were held in Toronto, one being on burial, and the other on marriage.

In 1975, a conference on "Celebrating the Word" was held at McMaster Divinity College and McMaster University in Hamilton, Ontario. The speakers were from the Roman Catholic Church, the Presbyterian Church of Canada, the Anglican Church of Canada, and the Reformed Church of America.

Unfortunately the excitement which was generated during this conference cannot be communicated through the written word. However, as the conference progressed, it almost appeared as if there had been collusion among the speakers, in that the inter-relation between the liturgy of the word and the liturgy of the sacrament became an underlying theme. The ecumenical dimensions of our dialogue became more and more apparent as those from the Catholic tradition re-examined attitudes toward the importance of the celebration of the word, and those of the Reform tradition re-examined attitudes toward the separation of the liturgy of the word from the liturgy of the sacrament. Father Diekmann, the keynote speaker, gave the direction when he changed the title of the symposium from "Celebrating the Word" to "The Celebrating Word." When we gather in worship, we are united in Christ in the praise of the Father, which praise is given in manifold form.

# Celebrating the Word

*Godfrey Diekmann*

I am deeply honoured by the invitation to address this national Canadian Liturgical Symposium. The fact that meetings such as this, in which all who call themselves Christians can now come together in order, humbly and prayerfully, to enquire into and to share their insights about worshipping God in more godlike spirit and truth, is itself a sign of the times for which all of us must be profoundly grateful.

I accepted the invitation to speak to you because I share your conviction that the theme of your deliberations these days, "Celebrating the Word," is of key significance in our common liturgical hope and program. And yet in the course of the past few months, as I mulled over the talk I was to give, I must in all honesty confess that my happiness about accepting your kind invitation sharply decreased. As a matter of fact I became quite nervous about it. For it became ever clearer to me that, precisely because of the key importance of the topic for any sound liturgical renewal, I would have to treat it not in its obvious and immediate import, such as is being profitably and widely discussed today in both scriptural and liturgical circles, but in a manner which you quite probably did not have in mind when you asked me to speak. In other words, I may be here under false pretenses. So I must at the outset beg your indulgence, and ask you to suspend initial judgement and hear me out with Christian goodwill.

The reason for my uneasiness about the theme. The history of liturgy and liturgical practice (and of Christian doctrine, too, for that matter) could be written in terms of imbalances: when new or rediscovered and doubtlessly important insights or emphases were warmly embraced and highlighted, they became more or less removed from their roots or total context, and therefore not only threw the whole picture out of focus but were in danger of losing their own true meaning and value. They themselves became distorted and even proved to be a serious disservice to their original excellent goal.

Some well-known instances. The most far-reaching such imbalance, I personally believe, resulted from the Council of Nicea's definition of the consubstantiality of the Son (the homoousios). No one will dispute its necessity at the time. But what became a one-sided stress on the divinity of Christ weakened disastrously the understanding of the fuller implications of his true humanity, especially in terms of the mediatorship of the man-God, our high priest and brother, who leads us in prayer and worship to the Father.

Liturgically this emphasis on Christ's transcendence inexorably led to many of the practices that became dominant in Christian worship during a thousand years or more. In fact some of them are still with us in our own day. To cite a few: the clericalisation of the church itself, and the clericalisation of its worship; the consequent undermining of the doctrine of the general priesthood and the practical disappearance of lay participation; the infrequent reception of Communion; the proliferation and excesses of worship of Mary and the saints, who in practical Christian devotion, if not in doctrinal principle, often substituted for, instead of illustrated, the absolutely unique mediatorship of Christ. In our own day, of course, the pendulum has swung so swiftly and far to the contrary emphasis on immanence and its catchword of relevance, that not a few concerned Christians believe that a recovery of the sense of the sacred, of awe, of mystery, of the numinous, is the greatest single need in Western Christian liturgy today. And I am inclined to agree with them. But I also believe that James Hitchcock misreads history when in his recent book, *The Recovery of the Sacred*, he states that the purpose of what he calls the "classical liturgical movement" of modern times (by which he means the pre-Vatican II liturgical renewal in the Catholic church) was to stress and safeguard the transcendent. Safeguard, yes; stress, definitely no! Liturgy had been suffering for fourteen hundred years from a surfeit of transcendence. I'd be willing to defend the thesis that, in the last analysis, the pastoral liturgical movement of the twentieth century was an effort to restore immanence to the scene, in other words, to achieve a balance, a dynamic and spiritually fruitful interrelation, between the two equally essential foundations of true Christian worship, transcendence and immanence. The fault of Hitchcock and others like him is that they have a short memory. But they are right, very right, in reminding us that, in the last decade or so, the too enthusiastic propagation of immanence, of humanisation, has gotten out of hand, is perilously close to secularism, and therefore threatening the very possibility of true worship. Our traditional over-stress on transcendence may have distorted Christian liturgy. I believe that immanence, at the expense of transcendence, is far worse, for it empties liturgy of all substance.

Another instance. When Berengarius in the eleventh century questioned the reality of Christ's body and blood in the eucharistic mystery, the resultant orthodox reaction, a vast and profound wave of devotion to what came to be called the "real presence," made the Eucharist in the popular mind something static, a presence, a Person to be adored, rather than a food to be eaten and an action of common worship. The altar, instead of being a table of sacrifice and meal, became a tabernacle throne for Jesus the Lord, and Benediction with the Blessed Sacrament was often more highly esteemed and certainly better understood than the eucharistic action that preceded it. Adoration, a legitimate, theological *deduction* and development from the scriptural data, had in popular practice become dominant, had seriously overshadowed, certainly devotionally, the primary raison d'être of the Eucharist as evidenced in revelation.

Or again, the medieval formulation of the principle of *ex opere operato*, "by the work performed," in regard to the sacraments was a happy refutation of the temptation endemic in Western Christianity to the many forms of pelagianism. The sacraments, it declares, derive no efficacy whatsoever from human merit; they are the actions of Christ; They are effective only because they are the word of God, in visible ritual form, deriving from Christ himself, and demanding our response in faith. *Opus operatum*, in ultimate analysis, was another more pointed manner of restating Saint Augustine's and the patristic description of sacraments as *sacramenta fidei*, as signs of faith.

And yet, by the time of the Reformation, the thoroughly sound principle that sacraments effect what they signify (understood as described above) had fallen victim, certainly in popular understanding, to the very pelagianism which it had tried to overcome. Sacraments had come to mean almost automatic dispensers of grace. They were viewed as *things*, valuable and powerful more or less in their own right, as actions to be performed by man guaranteeing him salvation. The line between this and superstition or magic was thin indeed. A good and needed principle had become so stressed that it had largely lost its roots and matrix. It had clearly become too isolated from its intrinsic and essential relation to *faith* so that, until quite recently—I would say until twenty years ago—it was a commonplace to speak of Catholics believing they were saved by sacraments, whereas Protestants held that man was saved by faith. The misunderstood *opus operatum* had similarly weakened the sacraments' living relationship to Christ, operative in the present, for they came to be regarded as things consisting of matter and form, rather than actions of Christ. As a consequence, the declaration of Vatican II concerning the real and active presence of Christ in the sacraments came as a great surprise to many. "Real presence" had been thought of only as regards the real presence of Christ in the Eucharist.

But why remind you tonight of these old horror stories? What have they to do with our theme of celebrating the Word? I suppose what I'm really trying to bring home to you, even at the risk of citing historical precedents in perhaps too great detail, is the liturgical equivalent of a basic principle of hermeneutics, that no text can be rightly understood except in the light of its context. In liturgical renewal, no single insight or goal may be pursued without safeguarding living continuity with its roots, and in due balance with other provenly valid objectives.

The reason you and I are attending this meeting is our conviction that celebrating the Word, learning how to do so, for the spiritual welfare of man and the greater glory of God, has high priority in renewing true Christian worship. We also know that in its contemporary dimensions it constitutes, in the program of our modern liturgical restoration, nothing less than a quite recent rediscovery of ancient and biblical values and principles. I seriously doubt whether the phrase, "celebrating the Word," which now seems so obvious to us and so imperative as an objective, can be found in any of the liturgical literature of, say, twenty years ago.

But already it seems to me—and I'm not usually a prophet of gloom; by nature, I'm an optimist—the phrase is in danger of becoming a slogan. What it stands for is being embraced, not only enthusiastically, but often unthinkingly, in undue isolation from the biblical and theological roots which would ensure its soundness and fruitfulness. Celebration! Wonderful! We're all for it. And now especially since we have rediscovered, as it were, the resurrection mystery and all the great positive glad tidings of our salvation, we can't have too much of it. So bring out the banners. And at least fifty percent must have the word JOY on them in prominent letters, and the other fifty percent equally divided between PEACE and LOVE. Unless we can make each Sunday service a Christmas and Easter and Fourth of July all rolled into one, we have failed as liturgists.

And I'm only half joking. Speaking only of what I know, in not a few Catholic circles, celebration has become not a servant of true liturgy but a tyrant. Understood in a secular, purely psychological sense, it makes ever escalating and ultimately self-defeating demands of so-called relevance, of adaptation, of experimentation—all in order to raise the adrenalin in the bloodstream and make the hearts of the worshippers beat faster. And so in consequence, since the mass is of its nature a celebration of *community*, if you're not in the proper mood to celebrate with others, don't be a hypocrite; it's more honest in that case for you not to attend

Mass at all, even though it may happen to be a Sunday.

Nor would it do much good, I suppose, to point out to such people that in the classical liturgical language of the Leonine Sacramentary the word *celebrare* means simply "to perform." Celebration equals performance, without any intrinsic or necessary relation to heightened heartbeat.

As to the Word which we are to celebrate, let me begin by making a humbling admission, echoing the repeated declarations of Karl Rahner, that we Catholics, certainly in the past several centuries, have not had what we could honestly call a theology of the Word. We are victims of the dichotomy between Catholic emphasis on sacrament and Protestant stress on word, itself a consequence, at least in part, of the *ex opere operato* controversy; and it is only the biblical renewal of our own day which is finally moving us to fill this strange and shaming hiatus in our otherwise almost overdeveloped theological disciplines. And needless to say, we have profited greatly from our Protestant brethren in our hurried make-up efforts.

I'm not sufficiently acquainted with the Protestant literature on the subject to judge whether your all-embracing stress on faith has protected you from something that is now happening widely among Catholics in their efforts to restore the Word to due prominence in liturgical worship, namely, the encroaching tendency to overly intellectualise the Word, to understand Word too one-sidedly as a didactic means, a means of teaching, of *didache*. In our enthusiastic recent sloganising of Saint Paul's statement, "Faith comes through hearing," we Catholics have even developed what I believe to be a mistaken mystique of "the word," understood, as it were, exclusively of the spoken word—as if the sense of hearing were somehow more spiritually adapted to the word of faith than our other senses, and somehow more potentially sacred—forgetting, need I say, that in an illiterate age with few books, speaking was the only means of evangelising available to Paul, and forgetting also what modern experts in communication tell us, that only about twenty percent of communication today is audial. But we continue to pin our hopes naively on an ever more perfect verbalisation of the liturgy. The rich and multiple liturgical world of rites and signs, the body and bodily gestures, the expressive use of things—not to mention eloquent silence—are being pushed into the background in favour of words, and more words.

To summarize. We shall largely defeat our high goal of celebrating the liturgy, and in the process also weaken and distort other essential liturgical goals, if we isolate the celebration and the Word from their roots and their profound biblical and liturgical history. If, that is, we pursue celebrating the Word in relative independence; if we, so to speak, absolutise both celebration and Word.

All of us are here because we are deeply committed to liturgical renewal. So allow me to invoke a principle of sound renewal in all Christian endeavour, whether doctrinal, liturgical, or whatever, namely, *ad fontes*, "back to the wellsprings." In striving to go forward let us be true to our sources.

To begin, let us remind you of a lesson from the Old Testament. The word of God, in Old Testament revelation and writings, was a word of power; it was the power of Jahweh in creative operation. When God spoke, it was not merely a fact of history; in a very real sense it caused history. He spoke, whether through salvific action or words, and things came into being.

And so before long among this early primitive people, a belief arose that there was a quasi-magical power inherent in the word itself. The word itself became more or less absolutised. For instance, the letter of the Ten Commandments and the legalistic observance of them became known as the "Covenant." Words substituted for what alone gave them life and meaning, namely, the covenanted personal love between God and his people, so movingly declared in Deuteronomy, of which the spoken and written law was an utterly inadequate verbal approximation, a mere hint. Therefore the prophets, inspired by God who is jealous in his love, consistently fought against this temptation of the people to interpret the word of God in a magical fashion. They never tired of reminding the chosen people that the undoubted power of the word is due solely to the personal power of Jahweh. It was not the word itself that had power and efficacy, but God who was somehow now present and operative in his word. Similarly, a prophet and his prophetic word have power for the sole reason that he is a prophet of God, a man whom God is here and now making into his mouthpiece and instrument. It is God himself who is speaking through his prophets.

But perhaps Christians, less than anyone else, have the right to be harsh in criticising our Old Testament forebears. For the "sacraments" of the Jews, the signs of God's presence in their midst, were limited to humanly observable events, or to spoken or written *words* that interpreted the events of their history. How were they to know with certainty that they were indeed the words of God? How were they to distinguish between false and true prophets? Yes, in the Old Testament the word of God, the spoken and written word, was the incarnation of God's salvific will. But the leap of faith, between that spoken and written word to the actively present but in-visible God, was so demanding that it was easy to suc-cumb to a quasi-magical extolling of the word itself, especially if assured credibility by the supportive evidence of the tradition of the fathers and ancient liturgical usage.

In the new dispensation, however, the Word became flesh and dwelt among us. The Word did not become word, the Word became flesh. The Word of God no longer was primarily a spoken or written word, which by faith men accept as the manifested creative power of a personal God. The Word was itself that personal God. In his fleshly visible existence he was and is the Word of God; and he spoke the glory of the Father, not primarily by spoken words, but by his very being, by his incarnation, by his saving and healing works, by his death and resurrection. By his spoken words he interpreted for men the divine power of his person, of his saving deeds; and spoken words too were words of power, because they communicated to men—made present to and operative in men—the saving power of his person and of his deeds. The in-fleshed Word could say, "He who *hears* me, hears the Father." But basic to that declaration was his other assurance, "He who sees *me*, sees the Father." The personal Word of God, the Logos become man, first and foremost by his human existence and redemptive works, celebrated the glory of the Father. Celebrating the word of God, therefore, we recognise now, more than ever, to be an important and indispensable activity for men and for the church of faith. But for a Christian, a man of the new dispensation, celebrating the word is a derivative imperative; its source, foundation, and lifespring is the celebrating Word himself. Jesus as the incarnate Logos, who was with us in the days of his flesh and who is with us still until the end of time, is himself the personal Word celebrating the Father, the person who, having united us to himself as the first of many brethren, now as the whole Christ is the celebrating Word for all time and eternity. One might even dare to speak of the meaning of redemption as the Logos, who from all eternity in the bosom of the Father by his very being spoke the Father's praise, in time becoming man for the one purpose of joining men to himself, so that we too now might share in him as the perfect word and song of praise.

Perhaps this may seem to be getting a bit complicated. All that I'm really trying to say is that, if we transpose the definite article, and instead of saying, "celebrating the Word," keep concentrating rather on "the celebrating Word," we shall have a far more basic and a richer theme which will moreover keep our present analysis in proper perspective, in vital connection with its source. Keeping the celebrating Word foremost in mind, we shall, I am sure, be less liable to distort or superficially empty the meaning of celebrating the Word or, to change the metaphor, to drive the latter into a dead end.

So, for the rest of this talk, I propose to show some of the liturgical implications of the celebrating Word for our professed goal of celebrating the Word. I leave it to others in the course of the symposium to address themselves more directly and practically to the immediate theme of this conference. All I hope to do is to sketch its broader and, as I believe, its necessary background. I hope you will bear with me if I call upon some of the earliest patristic insights and ideas as points of departure for what I have to propose.

1. The Word of God, the divine Logos, is the celebrating Word not only in the New Testament but in the old dispensation as well, in fact, for all and in all men of good will. Justin Martyr, the first Christian theologian, who flourished shortly around the middle of the second century and who centered all his theology on the Logos made-flesh, at the same time did not tire of telling his readers that it was this same divine Word who had manifested himself to and had spoken through the

prophets. So, too, spoke the great Irenaeus. For them, however, as for the generality of the other Christian writers of the first two and perhaps two and a half centuries, the Psalms were the chief locus of the Word speaking to men. A whole genre of literature arose which scholars now call "testimonies," but which, except for bits, has unfortunately been lost to us. Some of these collections of testimonies may even have antedated some of the writings we now call the New Testament. They were lists, chiefly of Psalm texts, foretelling the coming of the Messiah, his life and deeds, more particularly his death and resurrection. In other words, the Psalms were the book of prophecy through which the Logos spoke; the Psalms summarized the so-called law and prophets. Now it was probably only some time after A.D. 200 that the Psalms began to be used as the common book of prayer by Christians. They were still regarded as the summary of the law and prophets, foretelling Christ; they were still, and now more than ever, Christological, all about Christ, no longer however chiefly in the narrower meaning of prophecy, of foretelling the future, but prophetic in the doxological sense. This became the general patristic understanding of the Psalms, instanced most famously in the commentaries of the Psalms by Augustine and Chrysostom.

In subsequent centuries, too, the liturgical understanding of the Psalms was generally accepted. Witness the several sets of Psalm collects that have come down to us from medieval times; after each Psalm was prayed, there followed a collect pointing out the Psalm's Christological meaning and content. As Augustine puts it: each Psalm is either spoken by Christ, the whole Christ, Christ and his members, to his Father, or spoken by the church in the name of Christ to the Father about Christ, or spoken by the church to Christ. No doubt this manner of allegorical exegesis no longer appeals to most of us, but it spiritually nourished most of our Christian ancestors in the faith. And perhaps it's time we learn to distinguish between necessary scientific exegesis of the Psalms on the one hand, and liturgical usage and purpose on the other. Be that as it may, the Psalms in historical Christian prayer were not only ways of celebrating the Word but were primarily the Word celebrating. Since they were above all the Word speaking to us and in us, putting his words of praise to the Father on our lips, our response in faith had the firmest possible foundation, and celebrated the praise of God with the highest eloquence, because it was the eloquence borrowed from and shared with the Word.

But Justin and others, most strikingly Clement of Alexandria, dared to be even more bold in their understanding of the Logos as the celebrating Word. In his Second Apology, Justin tells us that not only did the Word himself speak through the prophets of the Old Testament, especially in the Psalms, but also it was the Logos who spoke in whatever true things were spoken by philosophers and poets and all men by means of their *logos spermatikos*, their reason, which was a seed of the Logos. All men, therefore, by the reason which God had given them, could partake in the celebrating Word.

2. The Word of God, the divine Logos made flesh, pre-eminently is the celebrating Word in and with and through his body, his community, his church. This is the great vision of Ephesians, chapter one. God has made known to us the mystery of his will, accomplished in Christ, to sum up in Christ all things in heaven and on earth. In Christ we have been appointed to give praise to the Father's glory. In Christ, in whom we have heard the word of truth and have believed, we have been sealed with the Holy Spirit, to the praise of the Father's

glory. That is to say, with Christ, one with him, we are privileged to be part of the uniquely celebrating Word, the living praise of the Father.

This vision of Ephesians was the inspiration of Irenaeus's brilliant theology of *anakephaleiosis*, "bringing all things to a head in Christ." Christ is the head of all creation, but not in a purely static sense. Not merely is he the head from which all men draw salvation; he recapitulates in himself all men. He recapitulated in his own life all the stages of man's life, all men's experiences. Hence Irenaeus argued that Jesus must have died only in his forties (which in those days was considered old age), because otherwise it could not be said of him that he recapitulated, and thereby intrinsically sanctified, all ages of men.

The story of Christ praising the Father is therefore the story of Christ *and* his body, through time, giving praise. It is the story of the total Christ, of Christ *becoming*, through us his members, the celebrating Word. We complete Christ as the celebrating Word.

I have just read a recent study by Jerome Kodell of Subiaco Abbey in Arkansas, entitled "The Word of God Grew" (in *Biblica*, 1974), which supports this understanding of the celebrating Word on the basis of the Acts of the Apostles. He exegetes three texts that serve as summaries of the early church's growth: Acts 6:7, 12:34 and 19:20. All of them have been, as he says, perennial sources of puzzlement for interpreters and translators. Each text contains the unusual formula, "The word of God (or of the Lord) grew." Now all agree that Luke was speaking of the community of the church growing; and there were perfectly good words to express "church" or "community:" *ecclesia, laos, plethos*. Why then use a puzzling phrase, "the word of God grew?" Kodell shows that Luke had a theological purpose in mind. He understood "word" in its intrinsic covenant relation to, and embodiment in, the Christian community. Kodell writes: "After the resurrection, the word of God is embedded in the Christian community. It lives in the church, in a community of life, with the believers. Luke sees the word (of God) so bound up with community life and witness (and I would add, with the community's great task of witnessing through worship, through praise of the Father) that he can say 'the word of God grew' when the church adds new members." Stating this succinctly, the church, the Christian community, is both the place where pre-eminently the Word of God celebrates, and even more basically, its highest dignity is itself to be mystically but really a co-agent of the celebrating Word.

This would hold true, then, of all who gather for Christian worship. But with special force it applies to those who have been called to be ministers of the Word. Both scripture and the fathers consider it almost blasphemy for a priest or any minister of the Word presuming to preach the Word while himself contradicting it by an unworthy life. For his celebration of the Word is then in unholy contradiction to his exalted dignity of himself being, by participation, the celebrating Word.

We know how obvious this seemed to the early centuries, leading in fact to the long and bitter Donatist controversy, especially in the African church. How could an unholy minister validly celebrate the sacrifice of praise of the all-holy One? How could he who is without the Spirit confer the Spirit in Baptism? It took Augustine to steer between Scylla and Charybdis and conserve orthodoxy against such persuasive argument. And yet, as the Reform theologian, Jean Jacques von Allmen, wittily remarked in an ecumenical discussion in Jerusalem some years ago, the Donatists may have been wrong theologically but they were oh so right pastorally!

3. The celebrating Word, acting in and through his

members and especially the church, must celebrate *in beauty*. We have talked much in the past about worshipping God with goodness and in spirit and in truth. The time is long overdue that we pay more attention to celebrating him in beauty, and not primarily for our own aesthetic satisfaction, but because the God we worship *is* beauty. The celebrating Word in whom we share is not just Logos as a prose word but Logos as a word of poetry, of infinite and beautiful song, forever singing the inexhaustible beauty of the Father.

Thus the second-century apologist, Athenagoras, riducules the pagans for their unsightly idols: they are shaped like brutes, and are ugly as well. God cannot be honoured by such as these, for God himself is beauty and fills the universe with his beauty.

Therefore, says Clement of Alexandria, we must now sing a new song to the Lord. For the Logos made man is God's new song—how often Augustine, too, uses this thought!—and because all things were made through him and in his image, he composed the universe into melodious order, so that the whole world might become harmony. The Word, the Singer, who is of God and of David the singer, despising the lyre and the harp which are but lifeless instruments, having tuned man, makes melody on this instrument of many tones, and to this instrument, that is, man, he sings in beautiful strain: "You are my harp, my pipe, my temple." Clement continues: "The celestial Word himself is surely the all-harmonious, melodious, holy instrument of God; and the Lord fashioned man after his own image, a beautiful breathing instrument of music. So let us sing a new song to the Father in harmony with the Logos, God's perfect new canticle."

That is how Clement begins his book, *The Exhortation to the Heathen*, and he ends it with one of the great hymns of ancient Christianity, one of my all-time favorites. Clement sings the praises of the Logos, the choreographer of the new dance, in which he invites his people to take part in honour of the Father. But they are often stubborn, often awkward. So the Word is "the bridle of untamed colts." He trains them to take their due and beautiful part.

Clement says it memorably in words, in poetry. Early Christian intuition immortalised it in the art of the catacombs. There Christ is often represented as a good shepherd. This is what one would expect. But he is also depicted as Orpheus, the handsome Apollo of the Romans, seated and playing his lyre or stringed instrument surrounded by birds and animals of all sorts, including fierce looking lions, whom he charms with his beautiful music and who are apparently raising their own strangely assorted voices to join in the chorus. They represent us. The new creation is the celebrating Word, is all who listen and take part.

A practical conclusion pertains particularly to the Catholics here present. The Catholic church now follows the practice of concelebration. But only the chief celebrant is told to speak the eucharistic anaphora aloud. That, I think, makes good sense; for choral recitation, unless highly trained, detracts from intelligibility. However, the other priests, the concelebrants, are directed to say the prayers quietly, which can only mean, to mumble them. I accept orders but, theologically speaking, I find no inherent necessity for the concelebrants saying anything at all; for liturgical collegiality implies—as is borne out by history—that one can speak and act for all. Moreover—and I believe this is just as conclusive an argument—mumbling, liturgical mumbling, is shabby and undignified, is unbeautiful; and a disciplinary liturgical rubric that inevitably involves palpable ugliness, is, I am convinced, unreasonable and wrong.

4. The celebrating Word is the Logos-made-man *and* all creation. The Russian Orthodox theologian, Alexander Schmemann, in a thoughtful essay entitled "Worship in a Secular Age" *(Saint Vladimir's Theological Quarterly*, 16, 1972), says some forceful things about the dangers inherent in some aspects of our contemporary liturgical search for relevance, in which we are constantly creating new symbols to capture the interest of the faithful. He sees in this an unwitting surrender to secularism, the most corrosive heresy of our times and of all true religion in any age.

Secularism, he says, is above all a negation of worship, not of God's existence nor of his transcendence. It is not a heresy about God, but a heresy about man, the negation of man as a worshipping being, a *homo adorans*, for whom worship is the essential act which both posits his humanity and fulfils it. It is a denial of the opening words of the preface found equivalently in all eucharistic celebrations: "It is truly right and just, always and everywhere, to give you thanks and praise." For the very notion of worship implies a certain idea of man's relationship not only to God but also to the world, to all creation; and it is precisely this idea of worship that secularism explicitly or implicitly rejects.

Schmemann pleads for a reaffirmation of what he calls the primordial intuition of men, that the world in its totality, and in its life and history, is an *epiphany* of God, a means of his revelation, of his presence and power. It speaks of God; it is a great word of God. Worship is based on this intuition and experience of the world as an epiphany of God leading to man's communion with him. Schmemann pleads, in other words, for a religious recognition of the sacramental character of the world, that viewpoint which finds such splendid expression in so many of the Psalms ("the heavens declare the glory of God") and which is found in nearly all religions, primitive as well as developed, down to our own time.

The world therefore is our means of worship, and our use of these means, of bread and wine and oil, of incense and flowers and light, reveals the inherent and ultimate meaning of the world, the fulfilment of its destiny.

The dichotomy between secular and sacred, which we have come so widely to accept, inevitably leads to secularism. In Christian liturgy, water is not removed from the sphere of the purely secular and then, by blessing or by its baptismal use, transferred to the realm of the sacred. Water, all water, can be called holy because it is a sacrament, a sign of God's power and beauty and love. Blessing water, or using it in liturgy, simply reveals more convincingly the fulfilment of water's intrinsic sacramentality. Liturgical word and sacrament are, so to speak, the intensification, the visible concentration of what is already incipiently present. They are the authoritative proclamation of the celebrating Word, who from the beginning of creation has been bringing all things to share in his headship of adoration to the Father.

Schmemann doesn't quote Tertullian, but he might very well have done so. For that ancient, doughty fighter in his *De Baptismo* sings the praises of water and its role in the salvation history of the Old and New Testaments. He cites scores of instances that have been echoed by many fathers and become enshrined in practically all subsequent liturgical texts. The Spirit, who is God's life and energy in all liturgy, makes all things new; he doesn't make new things. The bread and wine, by their being, always praise God, are always the image of God's bounty. But only if they are lifted up, become *prosphora* or *anaphora* in the eucharistic celebration, do they also become the food and drink of the table of the Lord.

I maintain that the old way of speaking still makes good sense, that the Word is the high priest, the mouthpiece of praise of all the cosmos; and our priestly dignity means sharing in his hymn of creation, being with him the celebrating Word.

We are most highly privileged to render praise in the Eucharist, *the* sacrifice of praise. What a pity that the canticle of the three young men in the fiery furnace, from Daniel, with which we formerly joined our voices to the whole range of creative things in praise of God, is no longer printed in our Catholic Missals. It used to expand our horizons, make us aware that in the Eucharist, as if in concentrated form, we were choir leaders of brother sun, of sister moon, of beast and flower, of water, wind, fire, and storm. Now one has to resort, apart from the Psalms, to the metaphysical poets—to Herbert, John Donne, and I'm happy to say, to the contemporary Russian poet, Josef Brodsky—to find the inspiration of beautiful words in order the better to fulfill our calling of being the celebrating Word together with Christ, and together with and in the name of all the works of the Lord. I stubbornly continue to believe in the celestial music of the spheres caught up in the Logos of God, the new and all beautiful Song who is still bridling us untamed colts.

5. The celebrating Word sings the praises of the Father and accomplishes his work in word and sacrament by the Holy Spirit, whom he is continuously sending into us and into the church.

For we do not even know how to pray except in the Spirit, who prays in us with unutterable groanings. All glory is to the Father, through the Son, and in the Holy Spirit. Jesus himself prayed in the Spirit, in his essential role as celebrating Word.

And yet, how we Western Christians have managed to

all intents and purposes to become "ditarian" in all but name, as distinct from "trinitarian."

For some years now I have been gathering evidence for a thesis of mine that in its early origins, every Christian sacrament, including baptism and the eucharist, had as an essential and usually predominant rite, the gesture of laying on of hands, of touch, which was a visual *epiclesis*, calling down the Holy Spirit. The accompanying prayer, expressing this in deprecatory form, indicated for what particular purpose the Holy Spirit was being called upon to come and sanctify. I am more than ever convinced that my reading of early liturgical history is correct, especially on the basis of the writings of Hippolytus as well as of Theodore of Mopsuestia and also John Chrysostom. Laying on of hands, the gesture of touching common to all the sacraments, was the external sign of prior and most basic significance. It was the visual Word, the sign of Christ present in his community, sending us his Spirit. In fact, I would even venture a new definition of the sacraments: they are the chief visible signs or actions deriving from Christ by which he, Christ, continues to send us his Spirit for the upbuilding of his church as a community of faith and love, to the glory of the Father.

There seems, indeed, to be a detectable correlation historically between our western neglect of the Spirit and the gradual disappearance of the liturgical laying on of hands. The bodily gesture too is a word, a celebrating word of Christ, and a word or a sign of the faith of the recipient. As Tertullian in his *De Baptismo* analyses the relation of saving faith and sacrament, the action of the sacrament, the rite (including the spoken word) is the external manifestation of the faith that justifies. It is integrally one with that faith, it's clothing, as he calls it, which the new dispensation has added to the old in accordance with the command of Jesus Christ.

It seems to me that the traditional dichotomy between Protestants and Catholics, in regard to priority of word or sacrament in the process of justification, need not have hardened into seemingly irreconcilable opposition, or perhaps need not have occurred at all, had we not launched our argument from these respective distinct starting points, but had together been true to the common point of departure of all saving word and work, namely, the celebrating Word, whose very person, whose every act, prayer, and spoken word is for the glorification of the Father through the sanctification of men. Perhaps it is not too late, prayerfully and humbly, to make a fresh start.

# The Biblical Basis of Celebration

*David Hay*

My subject is the biblical basis of celebrating the word as it appears in the liturgy—the Word which is read, preached, and confessed. Of course it is also sung, and it is part of our prayer, but these features I shall have to neglect because I cannot say everything on the subject. I shall have three major divisions. The first will treat of the divine word as given in the divine deed. Here is an echo of Father Diekmann's discourse. I am not too happy with the expression, "celebrating the word," because the basic task of the word is to celebrate the *deed*, and so I shall in the first place lay the theological foundation of this business by talking of the divine word as being given in the divine doing. Then in my second division I shall say that the first celebration of the deed in the word is the prophetic kerygma, which means proclamation or preaching in particular. Finally I shall speak of the consequent celebration of the word in the credo, the creed of the holy people.

## The Divine Deed yields the Divine Word

Let me start with what might seem a trite observation: God is a God who acts. G.E. Wright wrote an excellent book with the title, *God Who Acts*.[1] It is an antidote to the common notion that God is the God who speaks, as if the concept, "word of God," which Karl Barth in the one-sidedness of the Reformed tradition calls the superconcept, covered everything. You may have read Austin Farrer's satiric comment about German theologians who "set their eyeballs and pronounce the terrific words 'He speaks to thee' *(Er redet dich an)*" as if the I-thou formula were the one clue to understanding the Bible, although none of us is likely to claim that he has ever in his life been addressed by God just as directly as the formula seems to require.[2]

In talking about celebrating the word I cannot begin with the word. I must begin with the deed in which the word is imparted, with what the same Germans call *Heilsgeschichte*, "salvific history," if I may avoid the term "salvation history," because the word "salvation" suffers too much these days from the crudities of old-time religion. "We give thanks to you, God, we give thanks as we invoke your name, as we recount your marvels." "Celebrating your acts of power, one age shall praise your doings to another. Oh, the splendour of your glory, your renown! I tell myself the story of your marvellous deeds. Men will proclaim your fearful power and I shall assert your greatness."[3] "As we invoke your name, as we recount your marvels"—the revealed presence, the known presence is the word or name received in the works. "I am the Lord your God, who brought you out of the land of Egypt, out of the house of bondage" (Exod.20:2). At the burning bush Moses had asked God by what name he should speak of him to the Israelites. Now he has it. The name, the word, was finally given in the event. "I am the Lord your God who brought you out of the land of Egypt." That name, in a word, was Deliverer.

In the New Testament, I need hardly say, the same principle applies. The name or word is given in the event. "The word was made flesh." In the saving work of Christ the name-word of God is given in a new way, not primarily in general descriptions of his attributes but primarily in the particularity of the divine deed. As for Old Testament times God's name was "he who brought you out of the land of Egypt," so now at this new stage, with a similar historical particularity, his name is "Father of our Lord Jesus Christ," who brought us out of a profounder bondage (John 8:33ff). The Father is known in the Son's action in the flesh, and the Son is known as the Son of this Father. A hymn beautifully says it: "Jesus, Name of wondrous love, Human name of God above." In his First Epistle, Saint John gives us a remarkable echo of Exodus 20: "This is his commandment, that we should believe in the name of his Son Jesus Christ and love one another, just as he has commanded us" (3:23).

In both the Old Testament and the New, the name or word is given in the event with commanding power for faith, which must therefore also obey its law. In *God Who Acts*, G.E. Wright is very helpful in describing biblical theology as "recital" theology.[4] There is in the Bible little theology of our kind—general discursive elaboration of conceptual themes—but recital theology there is in plenty, and the term "recital" is a happy one, because it brings into prominence the fact that God's deeds, whereby his name, nature, word, design, law and promises become known and are celebrated, are the major subject of the Bible's testimony.

## Proclamation of the Word yielded in the Deed

Now, secondly, if the divine word in the divine deed is to take effect within human history—if it is to *make* history—a human agent must be present who is so inspired to discern and proclaim the divine deed and word that he and his people can act upon them and build them into the life of a new community. Conceivably, the Exodus might have happened without Moses. Conceivably, a succession of pestilences and natural disasters might have spontaneously led the Pharaoh to drive out the Israelites, making them, not for the last time, the scapegoat of others' misfortunes. But such an opaque event could not have ushered in the historical church of the following salvific story. The divine strategy also included a prophetic call. A man is prepared and duly called to be a participant in the divine work, a man who could endure as seeing him who is invisible and who could therefore be a mediator and communicator of the divine action and word. The story of Moses as we have it no doubt owes a great deal to kerygmatic and dogmatic development of the tradition, even to the point of construction of direct dialogue between God and him. We do well therefore to read the narratives with imagination and sobriety, remembering that they say not only that the Lord spoke with Moses face to face as a man speaks with his friend, but also that the nearest Moses ever came to sight of God was a glimpse of God's back in passing (Exod. 33:23). What is unquestionable is that the divine deed and word called for prophetic faith and vision, a discerner of the signs of the times, if the deed and word of God were not to return to him void. For this reason Saint Paul can say that the Israelites were baptised into Moses in the cloud and in the sea (1 Cor. 10:2). In the mouth of the prophet, the word in the deed became the word in human speech, and what the community recited believingly with him was confession of faith, creed, witness to God's mighty acts, as we shall see in a moment. Meantime let us linger with the crucial prophetic word.

Moses was the exemplar of a great succession. "The Lord your God will raise up for you a prophet like me from among you, from your brethren—him shall you heed" (Deut. 18:15). Moses is speaking. We must not think of these men as uniquely endowed to receive messages out of the blue from God, as if they were good examples of *Er redet dich an*! This naive idea lies behind the assumption that revelation comes as an unmediated word from God rather than in a deed of God. On the contrary, the prophets had to be in the "apostolic" tradition of Moses, to stand where he stood on the Exodus Covenant; only, now, each in his generation had in turn to discern the signs of the times and say how these changed times stood with respect to the Covenant. Thus an Isaiah, contemplating a captivity of his people very like the one they had initially suffered in Egypt, could prophesy another Exodus, another journey through the desert, now blossoming like the rose, and a successful return of the ransomed of the Lord to Zion with everlasting joy upon their heads. The first Exodus guaranteed a second. The Mosaic word of the first Exodus was discerned and proclaimed again by Isaiah as another Moses for another Exodus.

The New Testament situation was parallel, on a higher level of course. The Word in the deed, the Word Incarnate, gathered around him prophetic men who could be initiated into his secret, his new Word, and in due course blazon it abroad in a continuously traditioned word in which he was alive. Inevitably Jesus was himself the first prophet, the first Moses of his own deed and Word. He too had to stand his testing in the wilderness, when, having been baptised in his own Red

Sea, the Jordan, he came in a desert place painfully to grips with the truth that his fulfilment of the Law and the Prophets, that is of the scriptures of the Old Exodus and the Old Covenant, would not square with what Moses and his succession had given out to be the word of God. The new revelation called for a new prophet in a new dimension for a new era and a new covenant, whose passion, cross, and resurrection would be the divine deed in which the fulfilling word would be enshrined. That is why, as Father Diekmann pointed out, typology must be a method of reading the scriptures. We are trained nowadays in the technique of exegesis, but we must realise that the New Testament can not merely give exegesis of the Old Testament. Learning from Jesus, the apostles had to look at it typologically and declare that the new covenant was anticipated there, not in the letter, but "in the Spirit," and visibly embodied only in the New Moses and his New Exodus (St. Luke 9:31, 35; 2 Cor. 2).

A strange idea afflicted neo-orthodox theologians of a generation ago who thought that we could never get behind the apostolic testimony to the Person of Jesus. Their odd error was failure to realise that everything the apostles said about Jesus was dependent upon what he had first thought and done and taught them prophetically, particularly about himself. There was no Jesus "behind" the apostles. The Jesus of their testimony is the Jesus who imparted himself to them, before and after the resurrection. The absolutely critical human articulation of the word in the divine deed of the incarnation was the articulation given by that Word himself, and in order that the divine deed might be proclaimed and celebrated by the word to the ends of the earth, he chose twelve patriarch-prophets for the new Israel to be, under him, the foundation of the church. In this special way, he initiated his new

"Mosaic," prophetic, apostolic succession in the word.

How much the prophetic word counts in both Testaments can be measured only if we recall the paradigm of Moses and especially if we recognize that the Day of Pentecost was the first occasion on which Christ could be offered in his fullness to his people and to the world, and then only at the mouth of Saint Peter and his fellows. As Nygren helpfully remarks in his Laidlaw Lectures, there were two reasons why Jesus could not readily accept the name Messiah.[5] One was that he was not to be the kind of Messiah that Israel and the prophets were expecting. A deeper reason was that he would not have accomplished his Messiahship until his work was done and he took his seat at the right hand of the Majesty on high. The Ascension initiated the possibility of Pentecost, when, illumined and empowered by the Spirit, the apostles, now at last discerning the word in the completed deed, preached Christ in his fullness to the world for the first time. The prime glossolalia on that occasion was prophetic and kerygmatic, not inarticulate. In and by the apostolic word, the Lord could now make his saviourhood effective (St. John 14:12). It is the glory of the Reformation that it recovered the New Testament's theology of the apostolic word as a prime medium of Christ's salvific presence and action. The apostles, we are told, went forth and preached everywhere, the Lord working with them and confirming the word with signs following (St. Mark 16:20).

At last I come, after this necessary foundation, to the subject I am supposed to be handling when I assert that preaching is first of all a cultic activity. When we think of apostolic preaching in New Testament times we think of it almost inevitably as missionary outreach rather than as cult. That assumption is too simple. Starting again with the Old Testament we notice the difference that, apart from the Book of Jonah, proclamation of the word was an activity among the holy people. "Then Moses and the people of Israel sang this song *to the Lord*, saying, 'I will sing unto the Lord, for he has triumphed gloriously" (Exod. 15:1). It is noticeable that the song is more concerned with God's greatness and his victory than with their own salvation. Overcoming the alleged conflict between prophets and priests, scholars are now reminding us that prophetic oracles were normally given in cultic settings. So also was it in the New Testament church. "And they devoted themselves to the apostles' teaching and fellowship, to the breaking of bread and the prayers" (Acts 2:42). As one who knows a little of the exaltation that comes to a preacher proclaiming God's deeds before God in the liturgical assembly and not just addressing the human individuals before him, I am convinced that unless we have this primary understanding of preaching as a prophetic, cultic declaration of God's mighty acts among his people, we shall fail to discern its inherent role in the liturgy.

Vatican II adumbrated these reflections in the *Constitution on the Liturgy* but not strongly or gloriously enough.[6] The "charismatic movement" is also significant at this point, for glossolalia is pronouncedly a cultic matter, although I have heard one of its participants say that since receiving the Holy Spirit she has ceased to need the church. Her deviation is serious, but surely glossolalia can become a cult even in a bad sense. Even without sharing in the phenomenon one can say that its paradoxical effort to utter the unutterable points the truth that utterance is a natively human and creative requirement, so that celebration of the divine deed by the inspired mouth of a prophet is intrinsically called for in historical revelation. The divine deed must be prophetically celebrated in the divine cult.

As I pass to my next point, let me interject the remark that, if I were not now restricting myself to talking about preaching in general, it would be necessary to expatiate upon its role as prophetic discernment of the word given at one time in its challenge to succeeding and different times. Prophetic discernment in the Christian era is concerned, as it was in the era of the Old Covenant, with the presence, action and will of God in contemporary events, as interpreted from a critically revelatory base. Only the preaching-teaching office can discharge this creative, Holy-Spirit function, which is indispensable for the continuance of the authentic tradition among the holy people. This topic I cannot develop at this point, but it underlies the indispensability of prophecy in the living tradition if the church is not to degenerate into a museum.

## Celebrating the Word in the Creed

The recital theology of the Bible finds inevitable expression in creedal affirmations within the liturgical assembly. The deed of God brings the community into being and the community regrounds itself in its being by invoking the deed in verbal forms. It is sometimes said that creeds only arise and formulations should only be attempted when heresy calls for correction. As a warning against unnecessary dogmatic binding, that standpoint has its worth, but I think it is too oblivious of the positive, creative source of creed in the divine deeds that call for prophetic articulation. Certainly only what is essential need find a place in basic formulations, and heresy must be guarded against lest it corrupt the community's discernment of the divine deed which is the basis of its selfhood. But for spiritual growth and deepening, a positive unfolding of the character of the divine deed and its relationships is required. Recital theology must be elaborated into discursive theology, kerygma into didache, if the church is to do her duty by her doctrine, ethics, liturgiology, missiology and all the churchly disciplines.

To revert to the main point, we have striking examples in scripture of the enshrinement of prophetic discernment in creedal forms that enabled the community to grasp and celebrate the deed in the word and hold it faithful to its roots. The offering of the firstfruits in Deuteronomy 26 contains a well known one. The offerer of the basket is to confess his and the community's faith before the priest, recounting the mighty deliverance from Egyptian bondage and acknowledging that God has fulfilled his promise to give them the land flowing with milk and honey. We have here a very clear case of recital theology, the divine deeds celebrated in the articulate word. My Old Testament teacher in Edinburgh, Dr. A. C. Welch, used to call attention to the heavy and repetitive emphasis in this creed upon the expression, "The Lord thy God." The creed held Israel true to the faith that they owed everything to the Lord God of the Exodus—the God revealed in history—and nothing to the alleged nature-gods of the soil on which they stood. The Passover celebration gives us another excellent example of creedal usage. It was not only concern for religious education, although it was certainly that also, but basically concern for the authentic creed enshrined in the festival that led to the injunction: "And it shall come to pass when your children say to you, 'What do you mean by this service?' you shall say, 'It is the sacrifice of the Lord's passover, for he passed over the houses of the people of Israel in Egypt, when he slew the Egyptians but spared our houses" (Exod. 12:26f). As the psalmist says, "One generation shall laud thy works to another, and shall declare thy mighty acts" (145:4).

In the New Testament there are a number of creedal formulations of which Oscar Cullmann has given us a classic account.[7] I need not use up time in enumerating them. The earliest was, "Jesus Christ is Lord," which was the original baptismal formula. It soon took on a trinitarian shape and in time the church elaborated the Apostles' Creed, which thoroughly deserves that name because it is a recital of the basic apostolic kerygma. The creeds are kerygma before they are dogma; better, these are one and the same thing.

We have, then, ample biblical basis for creedal celebrations of God's mighty acts. Only desperate biblical ignorance can lead Christians to imagine that creedal recital is "vain repetition," for our faith should be stirred to the depths when we ground ourselves anew in the company generated by God's mighty acts. British Puritanism committed one of its gravest errors when it more and more abandoned use of the creeds in worship, and indeed of the Christian Year, in which also, following biblical principle, the celebration of God's mighty acts is enshrined. Unfortunately the view is widely prevalent in Protestantism, startlingly erroneous and unbiblical though it is, that a noncultic church is a more soundly biblical church. There is a great deal of work for the Canadian Liturgical Society to do, and it is by God's providence that this Society has been called to recover for Protestants a better cultic sense.

Some of you may wonder why, in speaking of the biblical basis of celebrating the word, I am not, though a Presbyterian, offering a long disquisition upon the scripture lessons. Certainly a great deal could be said, but in principle I have, I believe, said it all, for what are the scriptures, whether of the Old or the New Testament, but ample kerygmatic and creedal affirmation of the mighty acts of God, as to their very heart at least? They are, as it were, a writing out in longhand of the prophetic word and the creedal response. Admittedly other things are present in scripture too. Proverbs is a collection of gnomic wisdom ascribed to Solomon. Ecclesiastes, called The Preacher, is surely the preacher in a very Mondayish mood. The Song of Songs, upon which my hero, Samuel Rutherfurd, drew very heavily, can turn you on spiritually or voluptuously, as you choose. However, none of it would be there, in the canon, if it had not sprung up in the community of faith which is centred on the salvific history of the divine deeds to which the canon testifies. Rightly, therefore, what we call the historical books were classed in Judaism with the prophets. The scriptures are all prophecy, which is not just prediction, but celebration of the deeds by the word. That being so, it is more accurate, as I have suggested, to say that the canon represents in essence the two forms of celebration by the word, proclamation by prophet-preachers of the divine word in the divine deed and the responsive acclamations of the divine deed by the people in creedal recitation. The normal place for the creed in the order of the liturgy ought to be after the sermon as the action proceeds to the sacrament.

As a concluding observation I should like to offer a correction of one of those imbalances of which Father Diekmann spoke last night, and defend the centrality of the liturgy, not least in the church's ethical and social obedience. Much stress has been laid in recent years, both in Roman Catholic and World Council circles, upon the servant-role of the church and upon the ministry or apostolate of the laity. The church, we are sometimes told, is not an end in itself. It is here to serve the world, and the role of the clergy, it is said, is to equip the laity for their ministry, which allegedly is the real ministry in the world. The good element in this attitude is too clear to need reinforcement, whether it is on the one hand the Roman rejection of triumphalism or on the other hand the Protestant rejection of mere organizational success. However, the emphasis described can import a very serious reductionism if the doctrine of the church as the servant-church is taken as defining its essential role and the consequence is drawn that the world must set the agenda for the church. The ultimate issue can be a very low-ceiled, humanistic notion of the agenda. On the contrary, one must say that the agenda of the church, the things required to be done, must always be determined by the acts of God, *Acta Dei ecclesiae agenda*. The acts of God must prescribe the agenda of the church. Of course, God's acts were and are in the world and therefore the church's agenda will be in the world also, in the setting of the world, but only by its being the *church* in the world. To cut the matter short, the church can not discharge its mission in the world apart from its re-enactment of the mighty acts of God. World-history is salvific history and the spring of salvific history is now the liturgy. What is more, God's love and hope are for his whole creation, not just for man, and therefore the liturgy also is cosmic in its scope. "All thy works shall give thanks to thee, O Lord, and all thy saints shall bless thee" (Ps. 145:10). Our understanding of the church and the orbit of the liturgy must therefore be very wide-ranging, for the church is ultimately identical with the new creation, the very kingdom of God, and therefore very markedly *an end in itself*, the goal of the creation under God and for God as the head of all things (Eph. 1:22f). The answer to the anti-institutionalism of the sixties, which the servant-idea of the church was partly intended to meet, is not to downgrade the church before the world or to defer to secular man allegedly come of age and scornful of everything churchly. There are many signs that anti-institutionalism has pretty well run itself into the ground. The church has a unique, divine jewel in her cultic activity, not to be bargained for anything else, this pearl of great price with which to garnish and redeem the human scene. Only in the offering of the liturgy does the world find its destiny. The true service of the church to the world can not be accomplished outside itself.[8]

## Footnotes

1. G. E. Wright, *God Who Acts*. London: S.C.M. Press, 1952.
2. Austin Farrer, *The Glass of Vision*. Westminster: Dacre Press, 1948, p. 8.

3. Pss. 75:1; 145:4ff. (Jerusalem Bible). Later quotations are from R.S.V.

4. *Op. cit.*, pp. 43ff.

5. Anders Nygren, *Christ and His Church*. Philadelphia, Pa.: Westminster Press, 1956, pp. 62ff.

6. In conversation later, Fr. Diekmann told me that the original draft affirmed the "sacramental" character of preaching as fully as could be desired, but the final product was weaker. However, in a later encyclical, Pope Paul restored the full doctrine.

7. Oscar Cullmann, *The Earliest Christian Confessions* (tr. J.K.S. Reid). London: Lutterworth Press, 1949.

8. A final appendix to the above address has been omitted, which was designed to obviate another imbalance. The liturgy goes beyond celebration of the divine deed in the word. The climax comes in its celebration in another *deed*—the sacramental action.

# The Theological Basis of Celebration

*Eugene Fairweather*

I shall begin by saying that, to my mind, the definition
of both the title and the subtitle of this lecture requires
some sharpening. The basic reason is that "celebrating
the word" is an inherently ambiguous phrase. The ambiguity of the phrase "celebrating the word" stems from
the diversity in the use of the term "word" within the
Christian tradition. This diversity, I might say paren-
thetically, was very well illustrated in a fine article by
Professor David Hay on the term "word" in biblical
usage in the second volume of *Canadian Journal of
Theology*. Professor Hay, in that article, offered a fairly
detailed analysis and made some attempt at synthesis. I
think it came out fairly clearly that, when a careful
analysis has been made, even the most determined effort at synthesis leaves us with an irreducible duality of
meaning. On the one hand, the term "word" may refer
to divine reality, to the divine Word himself; on the
other hand, it may refer to the verbal signs which witness to the being and deed, the being and action, of the
divine Word. For me, therefore, the pertinent question
as I reflected on my task today was this: is my theme to
be the divine reality celebrated in all Christian worship,

the Word in whom the Father eternally expresses himself and through whom he discloses himself to humankind, or is it rather to be a particular medium of celebration, human speech in its various uses in Christian worship? Either topic would be a good one, and in fact I shall find myself saying something about both, but it is important to distinguish them and to know which one we are talking about at a given moment.

I can sharpen the distinction by referring to a parallel ambiguity in traditional Christian language. I have in mind the ancient phrase "celebrating the mysteries." It can quite obviously mean one of two things. It can refer to celebrating the mysteries of God's life, purpose and action, or it can mean celebrating the sacraments. Odo Casel, in *The Mystery of Christian Worship*, points out how even in Pauline language this ambiguity may appear, as when St. Paul calls the apostles stewards of God's mysteries. He means, first of all, the mystery of Christ which he proclaims, and then, in addition, the sacred action by which we are taken up and grafted into this one mystery.

I must say that I found my suspicion of this duality in classical Christian vocabulary verified when I undertook a little word study of my own—a limited study of the use of the terms *celebrare* and *celebratio* ("to celebrate" and "celebration") in early Christian usage. Being an Anglican, I tend to be rather hung up on the formula *lex orandi lex credendi* (the form of prayer establishes the form of belief), and also to think that it does us good from time to time to have a look at the patristic age. It seemed to me that I might usefully undertake a brief examination of the use of the vocabulary of *celebrare* and *celebratio* in the Gelasian Sacramentary, one of the great monuments of the ancient Roman liturgy. I found that there was a duality in the use of the terms in that document. One finds, for example, in the prayer for vespers at Christmas: "May they receive without end those things which in time they desire to celebrate." That is clearly a reference to the divine reality, the divine act and the divine gift. One can find a similar expression in the address given to the candidates for baptism at the time the creed is communicated to them: "In baptism a certain death and a certain resurrection is celebrated. The old man is put off and the new one is put on." There the reference is clearly to the participation of the person to be baptised in the mystery of the death and resurrection of Christ. Or again, one can find in one of the prayers for Easter Week a reference to God's granting us, with exalted minds, "to celebrate your Pascha" (Passover). That again seems to be a reference to the reality which is celebrated—but then one finds references to celebrating the Paschal sacrament. A bit further on, in the liturgy for Pentecost, one finds a reference in the preface to the fact that today we celebrate the coming of the Holy Spirit, but then a little later the priest says: "Celebrating the most sacred day of Pentecost, in which the Holy Spirit fulfilled the apostles and the company of believers with the presence of his majesty." Here the two usages appear successively: the reference, first to the mystery itself, the advent of the Holy Spirit, and then to the day, the solemnity, as that which is celebrated.

I think that the distinction just formulated is an important one. To make it, of course, is not to deny the real union in being and action between Christ and his body the church. It is not to deny that the Word bears witness to himself through human words, or that he effects his presence through human acts, but it is to remind ourselves that the incarnate Word has passed beyond the sense-experience, the hearing and sight and touch, of men. His historical humanity, the conjoint instrument of his divine purpose and action, is no longer immediately accessible to them. Now they must encounter the divine-human Christ through signs, audible and visible and tangible, which are not simply identical with him. This is true even of the eucharist where (many of us would hold) the union between sign and thing signified is uniquely close. As a familiar eucharistic hymn puts it, with reference to Christ's action at the Last Supper and, constructively, in every eucharist, he gives himself with his own hands. Nonetheless, the putative author of that hymn was also capable of making a very clear distinction between the outward sign and the thing signified. For example he sang, in a stanza from the sequence for Corpus Christi:

> When the sacrament is broken,
> Doubt not in each severed token,
> Hallowed by the word once spoken,
> Resteth all the true content:
> Nought the precious gift divideth,
> Breaking but the sign betideth
> He himself the same abideth,
> Nothing of his fullness spent.

There the distinction between sign and thing signified is lucidly expressed. The frequently quoted words of Leo the Great are pertinent here: "What was visible in our Redeemer has passed over into the sacraments." To put the point in the terms of the present discussion: the distinction between the reality and the outward celebration, between the Word who is witnessed to, and the word which witnesses to him, must be kept constantly in mind.

The context in which I have been asked to speak makes it clear enough that "celebrating the word" is meant to be equivalent to celebrating the liturgy of the word. Celebrating the word, then, is parallel to celebrating the sacraments. That is to say, I am to indicate in theological terms what happens when we celebrate the reality of divine life, purpose and action, through the medium of human speech. (I tried to sharpen this definition somewhat, in order to bring out a point which it may be useful for us to consider later—namely the duality in unity of the thing signified and its sign, of the thing expressed and its expression.)

And now, in order to set about developing the theme I suggest that we must put to ourselves at least three questions: One, what do we celebrate in every authentic Christian celebration, including a true liturgy of the word? Two, what is the meaning of celebration as such, and why does the Christian response to the divine mystery include celebration at all? Three, what is the special role of the liturgy of the word, in so far as it can be distinguished from the liturgy of the sacrament, in the basic pattern of Christian celebration? Thus the body of this lecture must contain three main sections: One, the content of Christian celebration; two, the significance of Christian celebration; three, the liturgy of the word in Christian celebration.

First then, content. Our first concern in considering Christian celebration must be to determine what it is about. Human beings can celebrate a vast range of things, human and divine, but what is the object that essentially identifies a celebration as Christian? Experience suggests that the right answer is anything but obvious to everyone. Take a popular current phrase, "celebration of life." That phrase is patient of many interpretations, few of them distinctively Christian, and some of them problematical. A celebration of life, for example, could be a solemn religious celebration of creation. That is just what Thomas Aquinas said that the Old Testament celebration of the Sabbath was. It could be a less solemn and less sober religious celebration of fertility. The prophets and the people of the old covenant saw quite a lot of that going on around them. Or a celebration of life could be a secular birthday party. Of course, Christians do believe that creation, sexuality and human personality are good, and they thank God for them, but the essential distinction of Christian celebration is that it celebrates one all-transcending, yet all-encompassing, life—the divine life revealed and communicated in Jesus Christ, the Word made flesh. Another way of expressing this truth is to say that Christians celebrate the divine mystery—the mystery of God's triune life and love, in which his purpose and action in nature and grace are rooted; the mystery of God's life shared with men, which is grace; the mystery of Christ, in whom the divine life is uniquely and definitively embodied and manifested. In other words, the content of Christian celebration is God's own mysterious life: eternal, shared, incarnate.

I think that Dom Casel—a somewhat dangerous person, perhaps, to quote on the subject of "mysteries," in view of the difficulties which both historians of religion and scholastic theologians have raised about his particular interpretation of the mystery-language of the patristic age and the theological constructions which he based on that interpretation—is quite unexceptionable in his basic description of mystery in the second chapter of *The Mystery of Christian Worship*, where he tells us very well what Christian worship is about. "St. Paul," he says, "thinks of Christianity, the good news, as 'a mystery;' but not merely in the sense of a hidden, mysterious teaching about the things of God, a sense the word already bore in the philosophy of late antiquity. Rather for him *mysterium* means first of all a deed of God's, the execution of an everlasting plan of his through an act which proceeds from his eternity, realized in time and the world, and returning once more to him its goal in eternity. We can express the mystery so conceived, by the one word 'Christ,' meaning by it the Saviour's person together with his mystical body, the church. It embraces first of all God's incarnation, which is his last and final revelation to the world. Paul says this mystery was 'hidden' or 'unspoken before the ages', because it lay in the womb of the godhead, unknown even to the multitude of angels; hence it is called *mysterium, arcanum, secretum*. But this mystery was revealed in time, by God's taking flesh from mankind, and appearing visible to it. It is a 'revelation', an 'uncovering' in the highest and ultimate sense. Before, God spoke 'in diverse ways and in diverse manners through the prophets', 'now . . . in his Son.' " It is this concept of the divine reality, active and disclosed in deed, in history, shared by God wherever his secret work of grace takes place, that I would like to have assumed as the background of my own assertion that the content of Christian celebration is God's own mysterious life: eternal, shared, incarnate.

It may be useful to develop this emphasis in relation to the theme of creation, precisely as a Christian theme. It is indisputable that Christianity shares with other faiths and philosophies some notion of divine creativity—most obviously, of course, with Judaism and Islam and with philosophies influenced by the biblical faith. Moreover, this community of conviction is hardly surprising, since it is a classical Christian conviction that the existence of the creator-God can be demonstrated—pointed out—through the created world. But Christians celebrate creation, not just as a religious or philosophical truth, but precisely as a mystery of salvation, as a divine act proceeding from the self-communicating love of the triune God, and issuing in the gift of grace and in the mediation of grace through Christ. Christians may hold—indeed with the dominant strain in both Anglican and Roman Catholic theology, at least, I believe they should hold—that the simple recognition of God as creator and the basic religious attitude of devotion to God the creator are an essential presupposition of the Christian appreciation of the mystery of God's life, God's grace, God's Christ. But Christian faith and, therefore, Christian celebration have to do with that mystery itself. Thus celebration of life, even celebration of life as God's creation, is not Christian celebration as such. What we celebrate is *God's* life, shared with his creatures, made in his image, who by virtue of their created nature are capable of receiving that life.

The heart of such celebration is easy enough to identify; it is the paschal mystery of Christ's death and resurrection. Through that dual event human life is effectively offered to God and transformed by his power. Through that dual event God's eternal purpose for humankind is proleptically but decisively realised and revealed. Inevitably, then, authentic Christian celebration focusses most sharply on the paschal mystery.

The view of Christian celebration which I have just sketched is amply supported by the tradition of Christian proclamation and worship from the beginning. Let us consider just four points for the present. First, there is the emphasis of the primitive Christian kerygma as reflected in the New Testament writings themselves. One could cite St. Paul's recitation of a kerygmatic form in I Corinthians 15; one could look at Paul's own account of the word addressed to man in order to elicit faith, in Romans 10; or one could speak of the account of the regenerating word in I Peter 1. Secondly, there is the fact that the baptismal event of initiation into the believing and worshipping community is directly linked, both in Pauline and in common later teaching, to the death and resurrection of the Lord. (Romans 6 is of course the *locus classicus* in the New Testament itself, but the notion of baptism as a dying and rising with Christ is one of the most obvious commonplaces of the Christian liturgical tradition.) Thirdly, there is the generally recognized nature of the eucharistic celebration—which, after all, is the central and constant feature of Christian worship through the centuries—as the *anamnesis* of Christ's passage through death to victory. Finally, there is the shape of the common Christian calendar, in which the paschal celebration stands out as the summit of the whole year's liturgical observance. My thesis could be further documented—indeed almost endlessly documented—from such sources as the New Testament, the church Fathers and the Christian liturgical tradition, but precisely on that account I cannot see that it really needs further debate.

I will now pass on to the second division of my theme, the significance of Christian celebration. Unless the main stream of Christian tradition has somehow meandered into the wrong channel, there is little room for doubt as to the essential nature of Christian celebration. It is, as we have seen, a response to the mystery of divine life and grace revealed in Christ. However, there are many appropriate responses to that mystery. There is faith, which confesses and accepts it. There is prayer, which lovingly contemplates it. There is theology, which reflects on its nature and meaning. There is love, which surrenders to it. There is obedience, which seeks to act it out amidst the responsibilities and demands and opportunities of secular human existence. What then, within this pluriform response to the mystery of Christ, is the point of celebration? Does it have a significant role in the Christian life?

Perhaps our best starting-point will be a simple description of Christian celebration. It is a liturgical action, a cultic activity carried out by the Christian community gathered for worship. Its principal components are two: first, the telling of the *Heilsgeschichte*, the history of the events in which the mystery of renewing and fulfilling life is worked out and unveiled—a telling punctuated by acts of prayer and praise; and secondly, the sacramental representation of the climactic acts of the same history of salvation.

But what good does it really do to tell a story and act out a drama? Let us stop and think for a moment before we jump to a false and unchristian conclusion. Can we assume without question that mature, sober-sided adults enjoy a monopoly of human and Christian wisdom—that their typical behaviour is the paradigm of truly human and Christian activity? There are more than two or three texts in the New Testament, for one thing, which tell against any such assumption. Are such childish activities as story-telling and play-acting really alien to the genius of the Christian gospel? I suppose that the standard reaction of the adult, who has mistakenly let his mind outgrow most things that children do, is that they are useless. But is the useful so obviously the primary human and Christian value? I suggest that, on the contrary, "uselessness" is the prior Christian category, and that we shall fail to understand a number of essential Christian activities, including celebration, unless we recognise and appreciate their uselessness.

The first step is recognition, so let us consider some obvious, but too-easily-forgotten, truths. What use, for example, is prayerful contemplation? What contribution can we expect from prayer in meeting the energy crisis? Or what use is theological reflection? How will theologising help us to solve the problem of inflation? Clearly celebration is not the only accepted Christian activity that can be stigmatized as childishly and irresponsibly useless.

But surely, someone will reply, you have made nothing of the case for celebration by that line of argument. On the contrary, you have made a case against prayer and theology, as well as against celebration. To recognize all these activities as useless can only be to condemn them. The argument then must obviously be carried further. It is not enough to recognise that certain forms of behaviour are useless. We must learn to appreciate them precisely as useless.

I believe that it can be done. I have said that uselessness is prior to usefulness as the Christian category. What can I have meant? I meant and mean something like this. The very existence of our world, our life in the world, and our hope of eternal life and joy in God, all depend on God's decision to do something useless. What use is the created world to God? What use is our life to God? What use is our friendship to God? God has not made us to be useful to him. He has made us out of generous love, to find our happiness in knowing that love and in returning love for love. That is why, in the final analysis, the useless things are the fundamental things in Christianity: the prayer of faith, the understanding of faith, the celebration of faith. These are the most direct steps to the knowledge and love of God, who created us to be his useless, but his loved and loving, friends.

Perhaps you find such high-flown speculation unconvincing—even though, as some of you will recognise, the basic notion is borrowed from a very distinguished, though very small, modern book, Hugo Rahner's *Man At Play*, a book which is well worth considering. Very well then, let us look at a creaturely analogue. Like our relationship with God himself, human relations also become a disaster area if they are based solely, or even primarily, on utility. A man may marry a woman to procure a cheap and dependable housekeeper, or a woman marry a man for the sake of financial security. What a caricature of a deep human relationship such a marriage is! We may cultivate friendships to help our businesses or further our careers. What a travesty of friendship such an alliance is! Marriage and friendship find their profound meaning only in genuine mutual self-disclosure and reciprocal love. It is in the play of love and friendship, in spiritual and physical intercourse, that human beings truly fulfil each other as persons.

I just used the word "play" to denote the useless, but vastly precious, in human relationships. My introduction of that word was not accidental. It happens to be the case that one of the great classical Christian images of God's activity in creation and salvation, and of man's response to that activity, is play. This is brought out beautifully in the little book by Hugo Rahner to which I referred a moment ago. Perhaps no other image could bring out so well the sheer joy of God's useless creativity and of man's useless response in prayer, reflection and celebration.

I want to call to your attention a rather obscure text in Thomas Aquinas which Rahner quotes early in his little book. It comes from Thomas's exposition on the brief work of Boethius called *De Hebdomadibus*. Thomas is caught up in the phrase in the text from Ecclesiasticus which he uses as his epigraph, "And there . . . play," and he says that it is to be considered that the contemplation of wisdom is very appropriately compared to a game, because of two things which can be found in games: first, the fact that a game is delightful and the contemplation of wisdom brings the greatest delight; and secondly, the fact that the activities of a game are not ordered to something else, but are sought out for their own sake, and this indeed happens in the pleasures of wisdom. And Thomas goes on to refer, a little later, to divine wisdom comparing her own delight to a game, in Proverbs 8:30: "I delighted day after day, playing before him." I find that a good text to reflect upon, as we try to think of the nature, not only of contemplation, but also of celebration. It may well be that the best way to describe Christian celebration is to call it a form of sacred play. In celebration, with all solemnity, not unlike the solemnity of children in their games, we play before God, in response to his play in nature and grace.

But something more must be said: Christian celebration is a very special kind of play. It is an incarnational play. We tell the story of how the divine mystery was embodied and disclosed in historical happenings, and we act out the story in sacramental liturgy, in order to participate in its reality and power and, through that participation, to be united to God and to one another.

There are two reasons above all, I think, why Christian celebration is an incarnational playing. First, such a playing is appropriate to the nature of man and of religion. Thomas Aquinas has a rather good text on this point in his treatise on religion (*Summa Theologiae*, IIa-II ae, Question 81, Article 7), where he explains why it is congruent with the nature of man, as spirit in flesh, that his religion should take on a bodily form. Secondly, the nature of Christian celebration as an incarnational playing is in full accord with the nature of the Christian dispensation, which affords a corporate, not an individualistic, salvation, and so requires moments, events, episodes, rites, through which the unity of the community is constituted and expressed.

I turn lastly to the question of the liturgy of the word in Christian celebration. I must begin with the observation that there is a dual pattern in classical Christian celebration, the duality of word and sacrament. We find this in the eucharistic liturgy itself, which, in its traditional form, from the earliest times, includes both the liturgy of the word and the liturgy of the bread and the cup. We find this pattern also in the duality of catechesis and baptism in the scheme of Christian initiation. However, I must add that there is a unity in this duality of Christian celebration. One may speak—and indeed I think that one must speak—of the "sacramentality" of the word, that is, of the efficacy of the word as sign and instrument of grace. And I think that we must also speak of the "verbality" of the sacrament (if I may perhaps invent a word), because not only does the sacrament as sign speak to the mind, but the celebration of the sacramental action includes a word, a word of faith, in which the church calls upon God in faith to effect his mystery.

Now if someone were to ask what the distinctive role of the word—the word as speech—in Christian celebration was, I think that I should try to develop the notion along these lines. I should begin by urging that faith is the primary Christian attitude. There is no church where there is no faith. (One of the classical patristic interpretations of the dominical saying to Peter in Matthew 16:18 is precisely that the church was to be built on Peter's confession of faith in the messiahship of Jesus. I do not think that this explanation could really stand as an exclusive or exhaustive interpretation of the text, but it is one interpretation with a long history, and the fact that it appears in church Fathers and in an early liturgical text indicates that the ancient church recognised the primacy of faith as the basic Christian attitude to the point of saying that where there is no faith there can be no church.) The truth is that, where there is no faith, there can be no reception of that mystery of God's Christ which constitutes the church. But it is the function (I suggest) of the liturgy of the word precisely to elicit, to focus, to crystallise, and to strengthen that faith of the community, apart from which there can be no fruitful sacramental celebration, no authentic participation in the sacramental mystery.

At this point I could go on to develop certain themes which have already been touched upon by my colleagues. With no prior consultation, Father Diekmann,

Professor Hay and I seem to have come up with many of the same considerations. I should want, like my colleagues, to stress the presence of Christ the teacher in the community, in the liturgy of the word, and to emphasize that Christ's word in human words is indeed the source and the continuing resource of faith. I should then, I think, go on to discuss the primary role of scripture in the liturgy of the word, and to speak, in the terms which Bruce Vawter has made current in his valuable book *Biblical Inspiration*, of the unique inspiration of scripture precisely as witness to God's deed, evoking faith. I should also stress the significance of the actual reading of scripture, not least the solemn proclamation of the liturgical gospel in the liturgy of the word. I should then want to go on to say something about the role of preaching in the liturgy of the word, and to point out how the embodiment of God's Word in the word of man extends beyond the reading of the inspired scripture, the solemn proclamation of the inspired gospel, to an embodiment—dare we say it?—in the words which those of us who are called upon to preach utter out of our own minds Sunday after Sunday.

I have to confess that very often, in my own communion, as well as in some other Christian communions, the theological significance of preaching has been played down, despite the fact that preaching is honourably treated in important documents of medieval and later tradition. It was not, in fact, left to a Reformed theologian to observe that the principal task of ministers, and particularly of bishops, is to preach; on the contrary, you will find this point made in a little exposition of the Letter to the Ephesians composed by St. Thomas Aquinas. And it was not only Reformed synods that asserted the role of preaching in the life of the bishop; on the contrary, a council which met at a little place called Trent, in the mountains of Northern Italy, said clearly that preaching is the principal task of bishops. Nonetheless, I do not pretend that Roman Catholic or Anglican bishops have always lived up to this affirmation of their common tradition—although whether John Knox was really justified in rudely referring to them as "dumb dogs" is debatable. As the church's history has actually unfolded, the Lutheran and Reformed witness to the theological meaning of preaching has been profoundly important.

I hope that I have adequately stressed the reality of the presence of God's Word in the word of proclamation—not only in the solemn liturgical proclamation of the scriptural text, but also in the words of the preacher. But in that context I must now voice a warning. The preaching which mediates God's Word must be authentic preaching, and the condition of its authenticity is fidelity to the gospel and to the church's mind in the interpretation of the gospel. No preacher has the least right to mount the pulpit, all set to declare his allegiance to the latest secular fad or disposed to demonstrate his independence of mind over against the agelong teaching of the church, and to suppose that, in those circumstances, the Holy Spirit is going to do anything to him except damn him.

Just one more point—and here I reflect what, in Anglican terms, I might describe as my fundamentally "high church" mood. However important the liturgy of the word may be, it is, I believe, essentially oriented to the liturgy of the sacraments. It is intended to elicit, to strengthen and to develop faith in a reality which is communicated in a different way—and, I believe I must say, in a fuller way—in the mystery, in those sacramental acts which, as Hugh of St. Victor said, in a possibly misleading, but a certainly vivid, phrase, "contain grace." It is, I believe, one of the disasters in the history of the Reformation tradition—of the Lutheran tradition in most countries, of the Reformed tradition in most places, and of the Anglican tradition through several centuries (and even today in many places)—that the liturgy of the word has been, so to speak, put out of its proper station, and that it has been habitually performed apart from the sacramental celebration, to which, in God's providential guiding of his church, it was designed to lead.

Let me conclude with three summary statements: First, Christian celebration is celebration of the mystery of divine life, shared through grace and incarnate in Christ. Secondly, Christian celebration is the play of faith, an embodied prayer. Thirdly, the liturgy of the word is evocation and confirmation of faith, leading to faithful participation in the sacramental mystery.

# Conducting the Liturgy of the Word

*Howard Hageman*

When I started to think seriously about this address, the question in my mind was not only what I was supposed to do but why *I* was supposed to do it. The only answer I could come up with was that I represent the Reform tradition, a tradition which, I may say, has always believed quite erroneously that when it comes to celebrating the Word, nobody has anything to tell us and we have much to tell everyone else. After all, the first person to articulate the Reformed point of view was Ulrich Zwingli, who believed that Christian celebration consists in the proclamation of the Word and nothing else, and rejected all other signs and symbols from ordinary Christian worship. In point of fact, he did tolerate a little warming up exercise before the sermon and a brief cooling off period afterwards, but he made it perfectly clear that this was only a concession to the weakness of medieval superstition inherited by his congregation and that so far as he was concerned, if the congregation gathered on the Lord's Day to hear the preaching, it had shared in the only possible means of grace.

Despite the efforts of later reformers, like Calvin, to modify this point of view, it's amazing how deeply ingrained it became in Presbyterian and Reformed congregations, to the extent that the "preliminaries" are matters that can easily be dispensed with while the Eucharist is a marginal celebration connected largely with the observance of Good Friday. The celebration of the Word is the preaching of the Word and nothing else matters. That is still our Zwinglian inheritance. But in the churches of the later Reformation, however, the liturgy of the Word was almost invariably prefaced by an act of confession and absolution. In all probability this inclusion of an act of confession in public worship was an attempt to deal with the Reformers' objections to the sacrament of penance.

While Calvin and Luther retained a certain respect for this private act of confession and forgiveness, without investing it with any sacramental quality, they limited its use pretty much to those whose consciences were deeply troubled and in need of some form of additional reassurance. For the ordinary worshipper, they felt they had found an adequate substitute for the sacrament of penance in the use of a public act of confession at the very beginning of the liturgy of the Word. Some models were available for them in the prayers for the private preparation of the priest at the foot of the altar before the beginning of Mass. Even though the language employed by the Reformers was totally different from that of any of these prayers, there may have been some parallel in their thinking between the preparation of the priest in the old order and the preparation of the priesthood of all believers in the new.

In any event, when one examines the liturgies prepared by the Reformers, there is this act of confession, literally as the first pop-out-of-the-box; but it doesn't take much reflection to raise some question about it. In spite of the obvious parallel between the preparation of the priest and the preparation of the royal priesthood, from whatever language it may be phrased, the prayer is obviously a statement of the sinful condition of the worshipper as he comes before the face of Almighty God, and a plea for mercy and forgiveness. If that be true, then it's certainly fitting to ask what has become of the Evangelical insistance of the Reformers, that sin and forgiveness are matters which can be taken care of privately at any time within one's own personal devotions. Is the worshipper supposed to save up all his sins all week long and discharge them in this weekly public act of penance, or is the liturgical confession on Sunday morning the summary in public of what has in fact been happening to him all week long? Possibly because it left questions like these unanswered, it's interesting to observe in the centuries following the Reformation the disappearance of an act of confession from Reform worship to be replaced by that strange liturgical innovation known as a prayer of invocation. When later this became a kind of catch-all opening prayer, it was certainly meant to be a prayer invoking the presence of God in the assembly. Here for example is a specimen from one of the Reformed liturgies of the eighteenth century:

> Almighty God and Heavenly Father, we have come together for the public sanctification of this Lord's Day, to offer unto thee our praises and our prayers and to hear thy Holy Word. Thou hast promised to harken favourably unto all those who call upon thee in the name of thy Son. We therefore beseech thee to look down on us in mercy and to purify our thoughts and defections that we may render unto thee an acceptable service.

This tradition of a prayer of invocation has lingered long in Protestant liturgies as the proper way in which to begin the celebration of the Word. Its weakness can be seen in the simple fact that it asks for something which must already be assumed if any true worship is to take place, namely, the presence of God. It says something about Protestant development that the basic promise of the presence, which reformers could take for granted in a single sentence such as "our help is in the name of the Lord who made Heaven and earth," had, by the eighteenth and nineteenth centuries, become so uncertain that it required to be the subject of a special prayer before the service could proceed any further. To be sure, it was never put that crudely, but the impression left by many prayers of invocation was that of a congregation trying to make sure that God would be present before it wasted its time with the rest of the business.

The insufficiency and uncertainty of the prayer of invocation was probably the reason why in this century, in the United States at least, the celebration of the liturgy of the Word has become afflicted with what I might call "multiple beginnings." Many a Protestant act of worship literally begins several times, with a call to worship, choral or responsive or both, a processional hymn, a prayer of invocation, and then in more recent years, back to a prayer of confession. Any one of these would be a sufficient beginning, but starting the celebration with the liturgy of the Word seems to me like getting over a cold; if one method doesn't work, try several.

I've already indicated, though passingly, that in recent years the old prayer of confession has begun to make its reappearance in our liturgies, but often in a very new form. The objection was that the old prayers of confession, by their general liturgical language, caught nobody. In fact, since they sometimes provided a kind of holy insulation against any real sense of sin, the designers of these new forms of confession have tried to be unmistakably specific in their language— I was about to say in their accusations. Just last Sunday I had tea with a Presbyterian friend of mine, a layman, who said he objected violently to going to church and finding a set prayer in which he was accused of not having paid his income tax. A sample or two may serve to illustrate the kind of thing I have in mind. I'm quoting now from a contemporary liturgy: "In our homes we have been moody and irritable and difficult to live with;" "At our work we have been afraid to think and follow only truth;" "In the church we have been so immersed in the details that we have lost the vision of the eternities." Or this, which I can take as a higher prize: "We rant and rave upon our little stages, we grab and search for popularity, material wealth, position, status; pride and petty mindedness creep in, jealousy warps our common sense; like a terrible disease it drips venom into our hearts to poison all unselfish love, to chase away the last thoughts of obedience to Your will."

I didn't make that up. I have no scientific information to study the effectiveness of this kind of confession, but I suspect it's not great. All too easily the worshipper can check himself out like my friend with the income tax. "I didn't do that this week; don't include me in when you say that; speak for yourself, Reverend." If each of us is going to bring his own private list of peccadilloes and failures to an exercise, would it not be better to couch the language of confession in the most general terms, or to make generous use of periods of silence, or to eliminate the practice altogether.

From this brief survey of ways in which to begin the celebration of the Word, it is necessary to conclude that most of the ways which have been tried since the Reformation seem inappropriate to me. There is one other possibility which I have not mentioned, and I must confess to some surprise at the Reformation's failure to see it, since it seems to me so beautifully the extension of the Reformation thinking about the real celebrants in worship, that is, the people of God. Christians, save in exceptional cases, have no need to wait until Sunday morning to confess their sins to their Father in heaven and ask his forgiveness. In that sense the act of confession at the beginning of the liturgy is in no way a Reformation substitute for the sacrament of penance. But, assembled together as the people of God on the Lord's Day, they are no longer a collection of individuals; they are a community, a community which has been called to a particular task, to be the church, to be the body of Christ in that place. Whatever may be their individual situations, morally and spiritually, as a church, as a congregation, they have much to confess. They have not been the people that they have been called to be. The words of the Anglican prayer book describe with devastating accuracy the life of the average congregation: "We have left undone those things which we ought to have done and we have done those things which we ought not to have done." Precisely! As a congregation of the Lord Jesus Christ, we have fiddled around with incredibly trivial business and have neglected or avoided the real demands of our task in the world.

An acquaintance from New York once said that the general confession is not there to help the average Christian remember how many martinis were too many, or how many dirty stories he told during the past week, but to make the congregation aware of its failure to be the people of God in the city of New York during the past seven days. In other words, I'm arguing that it's liturgically and spiritually fitting that before it hears the Word, the congregation should pause to acknowledge its unworthiness to hear the Word, much less to be its bearer and representative in the world during the week ahead. Since the Reformation came down so hard on the idea of the priesthood of all believers, I find it difficult to understand why at this point its liturgy retained the old individualism. Certainly the evangelical emphasis of the Reformation makes that individualism out of place at this point. If we are the royal priesthood then let that priesthood, like the priest at the foot of the altar, acknowledge its failures and beg for forgiveness before it opens the Word. Nor can I accept the so-called prayers of invocation as any adequate substitute. To me, they seem to be a theological and liturgical redundancy. We have the promise that where two or three are gathered together in His name, he is there in the midst of them. We need simply to gather together in his name to claim that promise, without begging and wheedling that now we have gathered together, he must come down and see that we are here.

Certainly the confession of God's people needs to be followed by some kind of assurance that, in spite of their failures, they are still his people. Again, this is not an assurance of individual absolution done publicly and collectively, but an assurance of forgiveness for the church. There are a number of scriptural possibilities here from the Old Testament as well as the New. As a bridge from this active preparation to the proclamation of the Word, we need some great hymn of praise and thanksgiving for the forgiveness and acceptance which we have in Christ. The "Gloria in excelsis" has been the traditional vehicle for this in western liturgical use and is certainly a very acceptable one, but there are many others including a number of the Psalms and many of the great hymns of the Christian centuries.

You'll forgive me, however, for taking advantage of this opportunity to say a word on behalf of John Calvin's views, even though I don't think it's really liturgically practical any longer. It was at the same place where the Latin Mass employed the "Gloria in excelsis" that Calvin called upon the congregation to sing The Ten Commandments. In Strasbourg, they were set to a spritely tune, each stanza of which ended with the refrain,

"Kyrie eleison." In his correspondence, the Reformer indicated the reason for this apparently strange substitution: "When it comes to giving glory and praise to God," he wrote, "any fool can stand up and bawl out, glory, glory; but if we really want to give glory to God we do it best by obedience, and of that grateful obedience the decalogue is a fitting symbol."

I think the suggestion is an impractical one today for a variety of reasons. For one thing, its invariable usage allowed for no change whatever in the way in which the congregation showed its thankfulness for forgiveness. In later years when the spritely Strasbourg tune had disappeared from use and its more sombre Genevan successor had also been discarded, the attempt was made to read the law or some New Testament summary of it in its place. However justifiable that practice may have been theologically, it was not a success liturgically, for the simple reason that something read as a monologue at this point does not have the same effect as something sung to a joyous melody. There's the further point that the average congregation, the average Reformed congregation, lacks the theological sophistication to understand what the law is doing here anyway, and sees it as an irrelevant liturgical intrusion.

All of this so far has been a lengthy way of saying that the celebration of the Word requires some kind of introduction. I have been suggesting that the best possibility is a sequence which includes the confession of corporate failure, the assurance of corporate forgiveness, and an act of praise for our continued acceptance as the people of God. Some word might be added here about the physical expression of this sequence. I realize that no two church buildings are alike in anything including their acoustical properties or their visual possibilities, but as a general rule, however, I may suggest that for this preparation to the celebration of the Word, the minister ought to be in the midst of the congregation symbolising that he, too, is part of the people of God in his failures and need for forgiveness. After this sequence has been completed, an entrance into the place of the Word—pulpit, lectern, or whatever—will have greater significance.

Before we begin to speak about ways of conducting the celebration of the Word, I should like to spend a few moments sketching a little theology of the Word. I do so because it seems to me to be a very necessary basis for any form of celebration. Even a hasty look at a typical Protestant liturgy, which is not a very celebrative thing anyway, will reveal that the preaching of the Word is less like a celebration than anything could be. That's because it's usually cast in the form of a lecture or an address, and thought of in that way by the members of the congregation. By lecture or address I mean that a man who presumably has some expertise in the subject speaks to a group of people, supposedly about a religious, biblical, or theological topic. We know that, in fact, the contents sometimes are not in any of these categories but we can let that go for the moment. In classic Protestantism at least, the exercise has had a heavy academic overtone, even to the doctor's gown worn by the preacher.

Now I have to say that, as I understand the Reformation in its concept of the celebration of the Word, it was not academic; it was virtually sacramental. I've often wondered why the Reformation was apparently afraid of its own logic and refused to speak of the sacrament of the Word, when in celebrating the Word we are dealing, if I may use the term, with a kind of transubstantiation. The words of a human being are mortal with all of his limitations, indigestion, quarrels with his wife and upset attitude; yet his words, by the power of the Holy Spirit, are transformed into the Word of the Lord, that effective force by which recreation and new life take place. When D. R. Davies wrote his little book on preaching and entitled it *Twenty Minutes to Raise the Dead*, lots of people thought he was being funny, but in fact he was being very serious theologically. If it was by the Word of the Lord that the heavens were made, it is by the same Word of the Lord that human beings, whose spirits are dead or dying, are restored to life, given new direction and new purpose and power. Naturally there are all kinds of theological and biblical qualifications to what I have just said which a developed theology of preaching would have to consider. I'm simply trying to assert that the primary function of the celebration of the Word is not, as has so often been assumed in the Reform tradition, catechetical or didactic—that is to say, its primary purpose is not the imparting of information. In the original sense of the Word, its primary purpose is edification, the building up of the people of God. This was Paul's problem with glossolalia in Corinth. The language of ecstasy may be good for the speaker himself, but it is prophecy that builds up a Christian community. What he means by that comes out clearly in the previous verse. When a man prophesies, he is talking to men, and his words have power to build. They stimulate and they encourage (1 Corinthians 14:3, 4). This is what we are celebrating: the Word that stimulates and encourages, and so builds up a Christian community.

If this understanding of the meaning of the Word is not present, then all attempts to design celebrations are sounding brass and tinkling cymbals. It seems to me that the great tragedy of Protestantism lies exactly here. Having burst upon the world of the sixteenth century with a forceful recovery of the real presence in the Word, in what seems to me to have been a distressingly short time, that real presence became a real absence, as increasingly preachers talked about something that was no longer there. Believe me, a real absence is the most difficult thing in the world to celebrate. Even though I have to disagree with him basically, I confess to more than a sneaking sympathy with the old Presbyterian elder who once told me that all this liturgy business was simply a cop-out for ministers who no longer knew how to preach. They reverse their collars, split their chancels, hang up banners, introduce chants and responses all over the place, simply to cover up the great emptiness that had once been occupied by the Word of the Lord.

Of course he was basically wrong, but if you have ever been involved in a celebration of the Word which, when all the shouting was over, proclaimed something as creating and renewing as "Life is Good," "Honesty is the Best Policy," or "Possibility Thinking Will Make it So," then I suggest the most appropriate form of celebration is to close the pulpit, banish the Bible, drape the place in black, and commission a variety of musical settings for I Samuel 3:1: "In those days the Word of the Lord was seldom heard and no vision was granted." Seriously, when we talk about celebrating we have to have something to celebrate, and that something can only come from a deep commitment to the real presence of Christ in his Word. Incidentally, although I've spoken in the Reformation terms which are most familiar to me, I have a feeling that this theology of the Word is increasingly an ecumenical reality in our time.

After that theological intermezzo, let us return to our main theme: ways of conducting the celebration of the Word. Although the Reformed churches have always been scant in the development of ceremonial, there are several forms which I think might be employed. Many in this audience, I am sure, are familiar with the custom in Scottish Presbyterianism which requires that the beadle bring in the large pulpit Bible at the very beginning of the service, before he escorts the minister to the pulpit. It seems to me that that custom could be revived as a kind of little entrance. My suggestion is that instead of its being brought in at the very beginning of the service, the appropriate place for this action is the one at which we have now arrived: after the preparatory act of corporate confession and forgiveness during which the minister has been in the body of the congregation. While the congregation is singing its Psalm or hymn of thanksgiving, a procession of the Word could take place, somewhat similar to the procession with Eucharistic elements which occurs later in the service. Instead of the beadle, time honoured functionary as he is, why not a little procession performed by the minister, the readers, and whomever else, bringing the Bible to the place from which the Word of the Lord is to be read and proclaimed. I am suggesting that in as much light and movement and sound as possible, we bring the Word to its place of proclamation.

There's a very small group called "The Church of the New Jerusalem," or sometimes "The New Church," one of whose liturgical customs is called the "Opening of the Word." As I have seen it done once or twice, there is in their church a closed Bible on the kind of altar which they call the sanctuary. Often it is surrounded by a number of candles, or sometimes there's a floodlight concealed in the sanctuary covering. At this point in the service, while the choir or congregation sing an appropriate selection, the minister opens the book and the lights are lighted all around it and above it. I wonder why a church which laid such a heavy claim to being a church of the Word, we of the Reformed tradition, have nothing comparable? We read and preach from the Bible much as though it were a telephone directory. It would take only a little rearrangement to adopt the above custom. But if we are indeed to be confronted by the real presence of Christ in his Word, surely the celebration calls for something more than the etiquette of a lecture hall. Either a procession or a ceremonial opening of the Word offers real possibilities here.

I should not like at this point to enter into a discussion of what should be read. The only thing, and I'm certain of this, is that there is little if any justification for letting the selection of scripture be entirely at the whim of the minister. That's a priestly custom we could dispense with. I know that the Reformers, particularly those of the Calvinist side, objected to the lectionary system, partly because it so completely eliminated the reading of the Old Testament, and partly because the New Testament was cut up into little disconnected snippets. Their substitute was the *lectio continua*, a single lesson read in course until the book was finished. We live in a somewhat different situation, it seems to me. For one thing, we have a new common lectionary which does include readings from the Old Testament and which, by working a three year cycle, is able to cover most biblical themes. My own experience has been that with few exceptions, and there are such exceptions, the old system of *lectio continua* is no longer a viable one in most congregations. Imagine two hundred and thirty seven sermons on the book of Revelation. I admit that the exceptions may be important ones, but my experience has been that they can be dealt with inside the framework of a lectionary system.

I must confess, however, to some reformed uneasiness about the traditional custom which reserves special attention for the reading of the Gospel. I should like to argue that the subtle implication that the Gospels are in some way more the Word of the Lord than other parts of scripture can land us in a variety of theological difficulties. You will have noticed that I designed my ceremonies of celebration to cover the entire reading of the Word. I find it uncomfortable to sit in a pew while

Isaiah is read from the back of a brass eagle in the corner of the church, and then to be asked to stand while the Gospel according to Saint Luke is proclaimed in the midst of the congregation. If we are to celebrate the Word, let us celebrate the entire Word and not a section of it.

In recent years the celebration of the Word has increasingly involved the use of readers from the congregation, a practice to which in principle I have no objection. On the contrary, I'm all for it, but we must frankly recognise the difficulties involved. Unfortunately, public reading is an art which our educational system does not encourage. God knows it's bad enough with the clergy, but when a variety of laymen with little or no experience are shoved centre stage and asked to read a lesson, the results sometimes can be sheer disaster. The drama, excitement, and wit of the Word are almost entirely lost in the monotonous muttering and peeping. If there are any clergy who are equal offenders, and there are, I include them in what I am about to say. We would never think of allowing someone who knew nothing about music to perform as a soloist. We do sometimes, but we would never intentionally think of it! Why should we allow someone who knows nothing about public reading to serve at this liturgy. I think the assumption is that anybody can read in church because he's gone to school, but I can assure you that's an unwarranted assumption. Instruction is not difficult, but I do think that those who are to participate in the celebration of the Word ought to be required to take that instruction, and that ample rehearsal ought to be insisted upon.

If the celebration of the Word involves three lessons, as seems to be increasingly the case these days, then each reading should be concluded with a short acclamation spoken or sung by the congregation. In the case of the final lesson, that acclamation could well be an appropriate hymn. In any case, the pious wish which so punctuates much Protestant custom ought to be avoided at any cost: "May the Lord bless to our hearts this reading from His holy inspired word, etc." There's a place for a prayer of illumination as we shall see in a moment, but this is not it. "Thanks be to Christ," "Glory be to God," or similar shouts of acclamation are much more appropriate to what we have agreed is the celebration of the Word. In general, they ought to be brief and elaborated as little as possible in order to keep some sense of unity in this act of proclamation.

That brings us to the whole question of the relationship between the reading of the Word and the preaching of the Word. There's a Protestant style which separates reading and preaching liturgically by a number of items in the program, and sometimes symbolises that separation by reading from one piece of furniture and then preaching fifteen to twenty minutes later from another. It's against that style that I should like to enter a firm protest. Anyone examining Reformation liturgy soon discovers that apparently no place for the reading of scripture was made. That fact cannot be construed as an oversight on the part of the compilers. They knew perfectly well what they were doing. Their point of view might be summarised by saying, "no reading without preaching and no preaching without reading." The Word of God, primarily and finally the Word made flesh, is not only the written Word between the covers of the Bible. Moreover, there were times when the Reformers came perilously close to saying that the Bible was not the Word of the Lord until it was made to come loose from the page, speaking to this people in this time and in this place.

I've not been asked to come here and give an address on preaching, but I fail to see how it's possible to speak about conducting the celebration of the Word without saying something about it, for the celebration of the Word is a continuous act involving both its reading and its proclamation. It is for that reason, incidentally, that any prayer for the illumination of the Holy Spirit should come before the entire act and not before or after one part of it. The Word announced by Isaiah or Paul or Jesus Christ is the same Word which is being proclaimed by his servant, the preacher. As Calvin once said, *Predicatio verbi Dei est Verbum Dei*, the preaching of the Word of God is the Word of God. The recovery of that deep understanding of what we do in preaching seems to me to be crucial to the whole enterprise which we have before us. As long as we live in a world, and often in a church, in which the verb "to preach" has become synonymous with "to scold," and the word "sermon" the equivalent of an "harangue," it's idle to talk about celebrating the Word. Other traditions may cover the question of liturgical renewal differently, but I often think the Reformed tradition has to come at it through the sermon, since that is still the central thing in the minds of most of our people. Somehow or other we have to learn to put back together again what years of bad practice have divided.

Now that I am a peripatetic and sit in a pew on occasion, and also listen to student preaching, I listen to some sermons which are excellent Bible lessons, excellent exegetical commentaries on the passage at hand; I listen to others which are basically good discussions of human problems, whether they be individual or social; but I hear all too little that seeks to connect the two, to make the Word spoken by Jeremiah or Paul or Jesus come alive to speak to this people in their situation and in their need. But what else is preaching all about? Part of the problem is sheer laziness on the part of the preacher, and I speak as an artisan of the craft. It is far easier to stitch together bits and pieces of our recent reading or our pastoral experience than it is to live in deep meditation with an ancient Word until it begins to speak freshly to us. If a sermon has not already been heard by the preacher, what does it have to say to his congregation? Part of the problem is a lack of faith in what we are doing. "Nobody's going to listen to us anyway, so why bother?" But that assumption, you see, clearly indicates the mistaken notion that it is *I* who am speaking, that it is *I* who must be heard and remembered. It involves completely the faith that *my* words once spoken are out of my control and now belong to the Spirit to do with as he pleases. Part of the problem is the preacher's inability to surrender himself to the Word. Clinging tightly to the pulpit he reads his little essay to the congregation, and so misses all the opportunity to speak to them directly as the bearer of good and exciting news. In good preaching, body language is an important element, indicating the extent to which the Word has again become incarnate and lives among men to speak with its healing and recreating power. It all begins, and I'm afraid it often all ends, with the preacher. If he has something exciting that he has to say and will not spare himself until he has said it as effectively as he knows how, the Word will be celebrated. It's of that kind of apostolic witness that our Lord's Word is still true: "He who hears you hears me." Up to this point I have spoken as though the celebration of the Word were entirely up to the minister. Let me now remedy that omission by stressing the faith of the people of God as a most important component of our celebration.

I suggest that the difference between an audience and a congregation is just here. An audience comes to listen to a speaker, a congregation comes to hear and share in the living Word which makes men new and alive. Perhaps the beginning of liturgical health for us consists in persuading what have become audiences once again to become congregations. As one device to accomplish that end, one which I used in my years in the parish, let me suggest the use of the lectionary as material for shared Bible study. Naturally, the whole congregation did not participate, but we had a scheme whereby the lectionary was the subject of study for a group of interested people two or three weeks before it was to be the subject of the Sunday preaching. I tried very hard not to make the exercise a monologue but a genuinely shared experience, and I can testify how greatly my preaching was enriched by this, and I think those who participated in it would agree that it enriched their hearing of the Word as well.

Let me say also, now that I have become a peripatetic preacher with a different congregation every Sunday, how much more deeply I value the role of the congregation in celebrating the Word. There's a kind of marriage relationship here in which we can speak to and understand each other in a way that no Sunday visitor in the pulpit can ever hope to experience. As a seminary president I still write as many new sermons as I can, but for whom am I writing them? I'm sure I do the best job on those occasions when I'm invited back to my former congregation. I can preach to a thousand people anywhere else and never bat an eyelid. After all, I'm not likely to be back, and the role of the "hit-and-run homiletician" is a pleasant one. But even after this length of time away from it, standing in the vestry of my old church and waiting for the final bell to sound before the service, I can still feel the nervous excitement of the desire to celebrate the Word meaningfully with that congregation of the people of God.

I realize that, by my logic, I ought to insist that the congregation stand for the preaching, as I do insist that it stand for all of the reading. In fact, in Reformation

times it did stand; however, the invention of pews and
hour long sermons pretty well destroyed the continua-
tion of that practice. But this certainly is where our
celebration reaches its peak. The Word of the Lord
which creates and renews is a living word and is still
being spoken. I realize they can be faked; they often represent a superficial emotionalism. However, I do envy
my black brethren the acclamations which so often
punctuate their preaching: *Halleluiah*, "Praise the
Lord." A couple of years ago I did a series of sermons for
a black Baptist ministers' conference, and the acclamation which I liked best was somebody who waved a
handkerchief at me and said, "Stop talking, brother,
and start preaching."

There remains only the question of a response to the
Word which has thus been proclaimed through reading
and preaching. Most of the time, that comes in some
form of affirmation: one of the creeds of the church, a
great hymn, or even both. That part of the question is
simple. There's also a deep sense in which the offertory
is a response to the Word. In response to the promise
which has been proclaimed, we bring our gifts as symbols of the offering of ourselves to be living sacrifices.
But I hope that I shall not be misunderstood if I say
there is a real sense in which the most meaningful response to the proclamation of the Word is the Eucharist
itself. If at the time of the Reformation men complained
that the Word had been virtually eliminated from the
celebration of the Eucharist, I think the time has come
when the children of the Reformation have to ask themselves in all seriousness about the elimination of the
Eucharist from the celebration of the Word. It's not a
simple question, but I should like to suggest that proclaiming the promise without the response of the
Eucharist is something for which Reformed Protestant-

ism has paid a heavy price in terms of its understanding of the church.

I've a final word to speak about the celebration of the Word, and I've saved it till last because it really should colour the entire action. When Dr. L. P. Jacks, the English Unitarian turned 80, perhaps in preparation for the next act, he set himself the task of reading the New Testament through from start to finish. When he completed the task he recorded his conviction that the central theme of the New Testament is resurrection, the immortality of the believer in Christ as risen from the dead. Here are further words by Dr. Jacks: "This theme I found everywhere present, both in Epistles and Gospels, either on the surface or beneath it, sometimes in the foreground with the full light on it, sometimes in the middle distance, sometimes in the background, but its presence whether in one position or another, always the unifying element, holding the parts together and making of the New Testament a unitary whole." I quote from Dr. Jacks only to emphasize a point I wish to make, and I thought that a Unitarian witness might be a little unusual in helping me make it. Although it contains many shadows, the ultimate message of the Word of the Lord is victory. That word has to sound clearly in all of our celebrations, and its absence damages any real Christian celebration of the Word. I certainly don't want to get involved in a discussion about the gospels of positive thinking or possibility thinking which have proved so popular in my country; but on Cardinal Newman's principle that every heresy is the revenge of a forgotten truth, perhaps we ought to have a look at them. Could they have mushroomed in the way they have if the church had been proclaiming and celebrating the Word of ultimate victory?

Celebration, it seems to me, has at least three reference points: it must look backward, back to those mighty acts which brought into being the community which is celebrated; but that backward look soon grows pale if there are not also present realities to celebrate, continued experiences of joy and victory; and finally real celebration must also look forward to the completion and fulfilment of what has been promised. It's this that the celebration of the Word is all about, however we may conduct it. Our ceremonies and our actions can serve to enhance it but they can never create it. "Oh sing unto the Lord a new song for he has done marvellous things. The Lord has declared his salvation, his righteousness has he openly showed in the sight of the heathen. He has remembered his mercy and truth toward the house of Israel, all the ends of the world have seen the salvation of our God, let the floods clap their hands, let the hills be joyful together before the Lord. He has come to judge the earth. With righteousness shall he judge the world and the people with equity; praise the Lord!"

# Celebrating the Liturgy of The Word

*Joseph Cunningham*

Because of the pressure of time, I have had to limit myself to resources at hand, thus the language and assumption of this paper may be more Roman Catholic orientated than I might have wished them to be under better circumstances. However, inter-dependence of the lectionaries of the major churches enables us to make reference to a common experience. Eugene Brand comments on this fact:

> In a few short years virtually all American and Canadian Churches will be using lectionaries more notable for their similarities than for their differences. This common approach was achieved neither because of official pressure nor as the result of inter-confessional dialogues but simply because liturgical and scriptural leaders in the Churches had become convinced of the value of such a sign. It is interesting to speculate on the impact of this consensus upon Christian unity. Already clergy of various backgrounds are gathering for common bible study in anticipation of the Sunday sermon. (Introduction to *Preaching the New Lectionary* by Reginald Fuller p. xiv)

It is an agreed upon fact that there are distinctions of roles and functions among the various liturgical ministries. Although the specific personnel for each function may differ among the denominations, there is only one who presides as leader of the assembly at a particular celebration according to valid liturgical principles. This may seem and in fact does contradict parochial experiences of alternating celebrants in so-called "ecumenical" marriage celebrations.

## Importance of Proclamation

Although the title of this paper is "Celebrating the Liturgy of the Word," there is only one genre of celebrating Word and that genre is *proclamation.* In the order of ritual, the written Word of God is transformed by means of proclamation to a living, active, announced Word which is designed to transform and effect those gathered for worship. Whether the media be music, speech, dance, film, mime, or sign language, the Word is meant to be and is in fact proclaimed. Anything less than proclamation is a violation of Christian liturgy.

Again in the order of ritual sign, everything which precedes, accompanies, or follows actual proclamation enhances it or detracts from it. Thus the sign of book as well as the location of book and the chair of the presider is never to be underplayed. To the present moment we have a great deal of difficulty convincing Roman Catholics of the importance of a single lectern in sanctuary design, and yet, chapter five of the *Roman Missal* is quite explicit in this detail. The reserved Eucharist, traditionally the center of focus, follows in importance all the furnishings of the sanctuary for liturgical assembly. Still, the chair is frequently hidden behind an altar in the rear apse, and a dual place is established for the readings to separate the lay person or lector from the ordained priest or deacon in function.

The size and shape of the lectionary and the reverence shown it must be consistent. Brought in procession, elevated, enthroned, incensed, and kissed, it can never be placed on the floor or casually regarded. All of these signs of reverent concern highlight proclamation as a lifeless printed text becomes the living, at times consoling, and at times disturbing, Word of God to his people.

## Receivers of the Word

The receivers of the proclaimed word are the individuals who have come together in an assembly, a church (*quahal*), to listen actively. The assembly of worshippers is ordered: one presides, each has a function, nothing distracts. Worship demands a unique state of mind and attitude of attention in the sense that ritual word is timeless and thus recaptures the events of the past while proclaiming a present reality. Hardly is this a reading exercise of history, neither is it entertainment; it is ritual.

Each one must be open and receptive to the word, ready to hear it anew for today and his life situation here and now. Phraseology and terminology must be alive and fresh. The words themselves must make an impact. I think that two very hard and uninformed demands are made by worshippers of different Christian traditions today. Both set up roadblocks to proper reception of the word.

The first demand is the insistence on a familiar scriptural text all the time. It would seem that, given the variety of competent translations available today, congregations should opt for different versions of the scriptures. The classical English versions continue to deserve all the accolades of cadence and language. Obviously they have been and could continue to be memorized by constant repetition, but we are forced to question their continued exclusive use in the context of liturgy. It is true other texts could also be so canonized for other generations but this likelihood is limited by variety.

The second demand is congregational insistence on a printed text for each and every member in the form of libretto or missal, and now the periodical missal popularly called "missalette." This dates to the twentieth century response among Roman Catholics to the Latin liturgy which forced them to have an English translation for the sake of comprehension. Unfortunately the missal was not discarded with the new Order of Mass. The vernacular pointed out the inadequacy of public speaking among clergy and the poor acoustics in many churches, while the new lectors were not properly trained for their role as readers. Presently, people are convinced that they must have the readings in front of them while the ministers proclaim. This makes for a good community reading exercise but poor liturgical proclamation.

## General Principles to Enchance Proclamation

It is possible to list some general principles which should be universally respected when one attempts to enhance or find more creative ways of celebrating the liturgy of the Word.

1. Respect the particular genre of each prayer and reading whether it be: opening prayer, penitential rite, litany addressed to Christ, song of praise, Old Testament, Psalm, Epistle, Gospel, acclamation, homily, profession of belief, or bidding prayer. Thus for instance, an opening prayer (Collect) which gives a sermon to God, or bidding prayers which offer thanksgiving instead of petition, or acclamations which are recited, or a litany which states motives for seeking pardon rather than invoking the Lord, or a homily which becomes a catechetical lesson—all of these fail to respect the particular genre of the respective liturgical element.

2. Respect the role of the proper liturgical minister

and make sure of his competence. The one who presides should not direct traffic, lead song, and take up
the collection. Twelve year old children should never be
lectors for an adult community, and every pressure
must be exerted to assure the competence of everyone
called upon for a public role in the assembly.

3. Respect the role and ability of the celebrant. One
who presides must never be asked to do anything he
feels uncomfortable doing. This is especially true when
dealing with services of the Word for children.

4. Respect the age, educational level, and Christian
awareness of the community. No liturgical innovation
can be sprung on people without a proper explanation.
This does not infer that older people are not able and
anxious to pray better using art and media, but it does
mean that their sensitivities must be considered when
planning.

5. Respect the discipline of the media or art form
employed. It must be within the limitations of the place
and the vision of the community. Just as liturgical music
cannot be played off tune or by an amateur, neither can
media be presented by an amateur or with faulty
equipment. Just last year I was anxious to use slides
showing ministerial service during the Mass of Chrism
in the Cathedral. It would have been a good opportunity to pray through media and also awaken conscious-
ness to its use. After consulting an expert I had to aban-
don the project unless and until shades could be instal-
led on all the stained glass windows, for the Cathedral is
too bright. If an art form or media cannot be used well,
do not attempt to use it at all.

**Preparation and Prayer**

One of the main pastoral-liturgical thrusts in the
Roman Catholic tradition is the sharing in prayer of

liturgical planning. Since understanding, proper roles, and involvement of all participants are key factors in worship, it is necessary that involvement begins before celebration. Depending upon circumstances, planning has degrees of ease and difficulty: one Sunday celebration with a single celebrant is a bit easier to plan than ten or twelve Saturday and Sunday liturgies with six or seven celebrants.

Although the logistics of the problem are not easily solved, the necessity of liturgical committee planning must be affirmed. This must be a prayerful event centered in the scriptures. A study of the texts, commentaries, and shared reflections will help establish theme and determine a direction for the homily which is relevant for the entire assembly. How the liturgy of the word is celebrated will depend upon the creativity of the planners and the art forms at their disposal.

Verbal expressions by way of introductions to the readings, formulations of prayers of praise and petition, nonverbal forms such as related disposable art, symbols as decoration or gift at the offertory, media, symbolic things (water, fire, incense, light, darkness, candles)—any of these can be programmed into the liturgy of the Word on particular occasions. The reaction of prayer-planning is two fold:

a. It makes a tremendous impact on those who plan: suddenly the given of ritual has been modified by real people. (One woman told me recently how good it felt to have her commentary read at Sunday Mass.) Somehow, some of the obfuscation and distance of the ritual is removed when my creative prayer is proclaimed.

b. It relates liturgy to life: what does the coming of the Spirit mean for me? The homilist should listen carefully to the faith discussion about the readings. He can evaluate the specific needs and concerns of his people. Planning sessions are prayer sessions when the Spirit is active among his people and the word proclaimed speaks to life being lived.

## Verbal Enhancement

Because the liturgy of the word is already so verbal, one should hesitate to increase verbiage with additional texts. However, with careful planning for variety, especially in the alternation of spoken texts, song, and silence, it is possible to introduce short verbal statements which will assist comprehension: a short directive commentary before the liturgy, at the greeting, before all or each of the readings can be effective. A need for this type of direction can be established by merely asking a number of people what the homily was about on a given ordinary Sunday of the year; a variety of topics emerges from the pericopes in the lectionary. Commentaries should not prestate the text nor deal with historical or exegetical problems, but they should create an attitude of listening.

Even the greeting by the celebrant should establish a climate of prayer. It is very important for the presider to experience what the congregation experiences before worship in order to empathize with them and direct them to prayer. I would insist that he be in the traffic of the church entrance as the congregation enters so that he can share the parking lot jam, the rain, snow, cold, or heat which is the immediate past experience of all. In a verbal way he must lead the assembly from where it has been to the action at hand.

In every instance the chief ministers—celebrant, deacon, lector, cantor—should be named persons, not anonymous faces.

The introduction of nonscriptural readings into the liturgy of the Word is usually problematic, mostly because of bad experiences and denominational dissent.

Romantic brides requesting their favorite love poem, sisters with their favorite spiritual author, catechists with simple children's stories prejudice many ministers against introducing nonscriptural texts. Yet a homilist has always assumed the freedom of reading excerpts from current news accounts and editorials; bishops have insisted that pastoral letters (even letters of appeal) be read even in lieu of the homily.

In no way can the liturgy of the word be totally nonscriptural, but neither must the liturgy be so inflexible that necessary nonscriptural readings must be added on, rather than substituted for one of the scriptural texts. *The Directory of Masses With Children*, published in December 1973, begins to recognize the value of the nonscriptural texts more by way of commentary than actual reading (cf. para. 47). One has difficulty seeing why, for instance, a genuine pastoral letter dealing with spiritual matters of current importance to the community, could not be substituted for one of the two nongospel Sunday readings. Where this letter will be read as a fourth verbalization in the liturgy of the Word, pastoral decision based on sound theological principles must be invoked.

**Nonverbal Enhancement**

The opposite of verbal is nonverbal, but the extreme example of this is silence. Quiet meditation, real pauses after the invitation to pray, reflection on the text just proclaimed, are all ways of celebrating the Word. If liturgy has run the gamut from noninvolvement to super activity in recent years, it is definitely turning more to silent reflection now. Again *The Directory for Masses With Children* reiterates this period of quiet even for youngsters (cf. para. 37, 46). It is possible on occasion to let the homily be a directed silence; a few short sentences of direction from the celebrant could initiate this silent prayer and meditation on the Word and life.

Disposable art, such as banners and other hangings, are easily created and can have a good effect on liturgical prayer. Planning groups can frequently create a banner which will capture the theme of the day and challenge the congregation before the liturgy of the Word. Banners have many uses: outside church (decorative signs with clever sayings); inside church (as seasonal hangings or additions of color); within a specific liturgy (as precatechesis for the celebration). These should be as nonverbal as possible but they should challenge: the crown of thorns on Good Friday, the flame of fire on Pentecost, a candle and a basket (when the reading says don't hide your light under a bushel basket), the numbers (50, 40, 30, 20, 10) when Abraham bargains with God. In the latter examples, the banner challenges, but the answer is found in the Word proclaimed. Homiletic reference should enlighten those not so interested.

Music of various kinds—congregational, choral, cantor, instrumental (ideally live but even recorded)—allows for variety. Besides the Entrance Song, Kyrie, Glory, Psalm Response and Alleluia (which are more readily sung although they should rarely all be sung in a single celebration), it is possible to sing every other part of the liturgy of the word (readings and all, except homily). Pastoral and liturgical judgements usually try to avoid changing worship into opera; so prayers, greetings, and readings are usually not sung.

Good planning will use music *creatively*: the familiar *Veni Creator* played very low behind a dramatic reading of the Sequence for Pentecost, a violin or flute meditation, a coordinated homily which concludes with a gradual crescendo of voice and music to an acclamation of choir professing faith in the message presented.

Dance which interprets a Psalm or prepares for celebration by movement and grace can be introduced. A single competent dancer, preceding the liturgy of the word, can point out and prefigure all that will happen. Bodily movement can interpret the inner spirit of man as he listens with openness, gives thanks, and praises the God of his salvation. In silence, or accompanied by song or recited text, one or more dancers can assist the assembly in prayer.

Drama or acting is used too infrequently. There is no reason why a parish cannot practise and even memorize parts, use costumes, even necessary props to proclaim a reading; could the put down of Zebedee's nervy wife ever be forgotten after good dramatization?

Mime too is effective: the prodigal son on a bare stage goes to his father for an inheritance, leaves in a blaze of mis-spent pleasure only to find himself lost and abandoned; he returns to an awaiting father ashamed but still loved. What words are needed? We all know the account and yet a good art form says it anew.

Besides the Passion accounts of Holy Week, several editors have divided the longer Lenten Gospels into parts for dramatic reading. Although it requires a text, the people's part in the Passion does get everyone involved—but an additional suggestion has also been effective: break down the individual spoken lines into specific characters. Distribute these parts throughout the church so that Peter, Pilate, the servant girls, are heard as distinct voices. The effect is dramatic, while the direction of sound does much to increase involvement.

Visual images can be projected during readings, meditation, and homily. Even films may be shown to highlight or comment on specific aspects of a celebration. Where a film or filmstrip and sound presentation is utilized, congregations must be ready for them and feel comfortable with them. A planning team must communicate, by means of commentary, how the media fits into the celebration. The celebrant must tie the entire liturgy together in his homily.

Slide images may also be used as background commentaries for readings of the scriptures, as contemporary interpretations of the Psalms, as images of life which surround us. Thus, word is visually related to the world in which we live.

It is also possible to interrupt readings for interpretation and application. This can be a dramatic presentation, media commentary, or even a soliloquy which immediately applies the word to a familiar event. We have used this quite successfully to interpret the mission of one annointed for ministry in Isaiah: "He has sent me to bring glad tidings to the lowly, to heal the brokenhearted, to proclaim liberty to the captives and release to the prisoners . . . to comfort those who mourn."

## Homily

The homily is recognized as an integral part of the liturgy. It must be an attempt to relate the word just proclaimed to life and to the Eucharistic celebration which follows. The homily is not a sermon, diatribe, or even a eulogy (at a funeral celebration). It should involve people actively and challenge both the minister himself and the congregation as a whole. Rooted in the word itself, it must also have its source in meditation as part of the daily reflection of the presider.

What is a compliment for a homilist after Sunday celebration: "that was a fine talk;" "it made me feel good;" "I'm not sure I know what you are driving at;" "what you said was very upsetting?" Although we do not set out to disturb people, fidelity to the Gospel must at times disturb, because there are many hard sayings in the scriptures and people even walked away from the Lord himself.

The homilist has almost no limitations in presenting the lessons of scripture except the limits of good sense. He is not limited by place in the Roman tradition; the lectern, chair (seated or standing) are most appropriate, but he has freedoms beyond this. The type of liturgy being celebrated should dictate his position. In the setting of many churches, seating the homilist in the chair can be quite appropriate, warm, and intimate on many occasions.

When a community is ready, dialogue can be engaged in, but it takes a skilful presider to pull together and summarize the different ideas that are frequently forthcoming in such situations. All of the media mentioned above can be used in homily, and these need not be restricted to masses for children.

Separated word services can be conducted for children, even by one who is not a priest in the Roman tradition. The children can then return to their parents for the Eucharist.

## Conclusion

The purpose of this paper was not to give recipes for conducting celebrations of the Word, rather it was meant to state principles of worship which allow and encourage a variety of means to proclaim. One must first know what he is about; the name of the celebration is worship. Worship takes place with ritual signs within a tradition. It reflects the faith of a believing community. Accepting faith, ritual, and tradition, one properly uses art, media, and one's own personality to convey effectively and thus celebrate the liturgy of the Word in different ways.